On the Duty to Keep
Faith with Heretics

SOURCES IN EARLY MODERN ECONOMICS, ETHICS, AND LAW

Second Series

GENERAL EDITORS

Andrew M. McGinnis Wim Decock
Acton Institute • USA KU Leuven • Belgium

Continuing in the line of its predecessor, this series publishes original English translations and editions of early modern religious texts in the disciplines of economics, ethics, and law. Representing a variety of confessional traditions and methodological approaches, these texts uncover the foundations of the development of these and related disciplines.

EDITORIAL BOARD

Jordan J. Ballor
Acton Institute • USA

Christiane Birr
Max Planck Institute for European Legal History • Germany

Stephen Bogle
University of Glasgow • Scotland

Alejandro Chafuen
Acton Institute • USA

Ricardo Crespo
Universidad Austral and CONICET • Argentina

Virpi Mäkinen
University of Helsinki • Finland

Richard A. Muller
Calvin Theological Seminary • USA

Herman Selderhuis
Theological University Apeldoorn • The Netherlands

John Witte Jr.
Emory Law School • USA

Zhibin Xie
Tongji University • China

On the Duty to Keep Faith with Heretics
Martinus Becanus

Edited by Wim Decock
Translated by Isabelle Buhre
Introduction by Tobias Dienst and Christoph Strohm

GRAND RAPIDS · MICHIGAN

On the Duty to Keep Faith with Heretics

Translation © 2019 by Wim Decock and Isabelle Buhre

Introduction © 2019 by Tobias Dienst and Christoph Strohm

All rights reserved. No part of this publication may be reproduced, stored in a retrieval system, or transmitted in any form or by any means, including electronic, mechanical, photocopying, recording, or otherwise without the prior permission of the publisher.

ISBN 978-1-949011-03-6 (hardcover)
ISBN 978-1-949011-04-3 (paperback)
ISBN 978-1-949011-05-0 (ebook)

CLP ACADEMIC
*An imprint of the Acton Institute
for the Study of Religion & Liberty*
98 E. Fulton
Grand Rapids, Michigan 49503
616.454.3080
www.clpress.com

Interior composition by Judy Schafer
Cover design by Scaturro Design

Contents

Acknowledgments   *vii*

Introduction: Confessional Controversy, Coexistence, and Tolerance: Becanus's *De fide haereticis servanda* in Its Literary Context   *ix*

Translator's Note   *xlv*

Abbreviations   *xlvii*

On the Duty to Keep Faith with Heretics

To the Reader   3

Theological Disputation: Should One Keep His Faith with Heretics?   7

1. Three Types of Promise: Gratuitous, Onerous, and Under Oath   11

2. Under Which Circumstances Is a Gratuitous Promise Valid?   13

3. Under Which Circumstances Is an Onerous Promise Valid?   17

4. Under Which Circumstances Is a Promise under Oath Valid?   27

5. Where Does the Obligation of a Valid Promise Come From?   33

6. How Strong Is the Obligation of a Valid Promise? 37

7. Do We Have to Keep Our Faith with Heretics in the Case of a Valid Promise with Obligatory Force? 51

8. Do We Have to Keep Our Faith with Heretics When They Have Been Excommunicated? 61

9. Do We Have to Keep Our Faith with Heretics in Marriage Contracts? 71

10. Do We Have to Keep Our Faith with Heretics When It Comes to Freedom of Religion? 77

11. Do We Have to Keep Our Faith with Heretics in Wartime? 89

12. Do We Have to Keep Our Faith with Heretics regarding Safe Conduct? 93

Appendix: Addressing the False Claims Made in the Little Book *Third Defense of the Federated States of Lower Germany against the Calumnious Reproach That We Are Disturbing the Peace* 105

Index 119

Acknowledgments

The idea of translating Becanus's *De fide haereticis servanda* grew out of a series of conferences highlighting the major impact of both Catholic and Protestant theologians on Western legal, political, and economic thought in the early modern period. They were organized in 2012 and 2014 jointly with colleagues from the Research Unit of Roman Law and Legal History at the University of Leuven, the Acton Institute, and the Chair of Public and Ecclesiastical Law at the Martin-Luther-University in Halle-Wittenberg. Special thanks are owed to Jordan Ballor, Michael Germann, and Laurent Waelkens for their intellectual and material support in organizing these conferences. A first chance to explore Becanus's seminal contribution to questions of contract law, in particular, was offered to me on the occasion of the thirty-fifth course of the International School of Ius Commune in Erice in November 2015. Without the invitation of Orazio Condorelli and Giovanni Chiodi, the directors of the course, my interest in Becanus's *De fide* would not have been raised in the first place. My gratitude also goes to Thomas Duve, director of the Max-Planck-Institute for European Legal History, and John Witte Jr., director of Emory University's Center for the Study of Law and Religion, for their continuing support of research at the crossroads of the history of juridical and theological thought. Part of the research necessary for the translation work was funded through the Heinz Maier-Leibnitz-Prize, awarded to me in 2014 while I was a research group leader at the Max-Planck-Institute in Frankfurt. It allowed me to invite Isabelle Buhre to translate the work. I also was

Acknowledgments

fortunate enough to discover that Christoph Strohm and Tobias Dienst of the Chair of Church History at the University of Heidelberg were willing to write the introduction to this translation. Their expertise in the fields of controversial theology and the connections between law and theology in early modern Germany is unique. During the final stages of the editorial process, the manuscript greatly benefited from Drew McGinnis's meticulous reading and careful remarks, as always. On a personal note, I wish to thank my wife, Aude, for patiently enduring my scholarly endeavors with faith and tolerance.

— Wim Decock

Introduction

CONFESSIONAL CONTROVERSY, COEXISTENCE, AND TOLERANCE: BECANUS'S *DE FIDE HAERETICIS SERVANDA* IN ITS LITERARY CONTEXT

Tobias Dienst
Christoph Strohm

Becanus's Theses and His Early Perspective on Toleration

The Jesuit controversialist Martinus Becanus (1563–1624) was one of the most influential polemical authors of his time. Born in Hilvarenbeek, North Brabant, he joined the Society of Jesus at an early age. In 1601 he was appointed Professor of Scholastic Theology at the Jesuit college in Mainz. He soon made a name for himself as an expert in the confessional controversies, opposing primarily Reformed theologians in neighboring Heidelberg and elsewhere. He became internationally known after attacking King James I and his Anglican defenders for the introduction of the Oath of Allegiance. In the ongoing debate, Becanus's opponents pressed him to elevate his order's papalist positions on the competence of kings and the pope in temporal and ecclesiastical matters to such a point that he faced condemnation by the University and the Parliament of Paris. In a vain attempt to prevent this public debacle one of his books was temporarily placed on the Roman Index.[1] Despite this episode, Becanus was able to continue in his career, was promoted to a professorship in Vienna, and was appointed imperial court confessor in 1620. During his service in this prominent position, he wrote his main work, *Manuale controversiarum huius temporis*, a

---

[1] See Stefania Tutino, *Empire of Souls: Robert Bellarmine and the Christian Commonwealth* (Oxford: Oxford University Press, 2010), 211–60.

INTRODUCTION

polemical handbook for the clergy published in 1623, one year before his death.

Becanus's *De fide haereticis servanda* contains theses of an academic disputation defended by his student, the noble cleric Johann Ludwig von Hagen,[2] at the Jesuit college of Mainz in 1607. The work considers multiple questions concerning contracts and agreements with heretics. Becanus begins with an explanation of the different forms of contracts and agreements and explains the requirements that make them valid. After establishing these general explanations, the Jesuit takes on specific questions concerning vital issues deriving from the coexistence of Catholics and heretics in Europe: Are agreements with and promises to heretics morally permitted? And in case they are permitted, is there a moral obligation to fulfill them? What about matrimonial contracts between Catholics and heretics? What about princes and other Catholic authorities: Are they allowed to conclude and keep contracts with heretics concerning religious freedom, military alliances, and safe conduct?

Becanus's argumentation is a moral theological approach that relies on the works of his fellow Jesuit Luis de Molina (1535–1600) and other authors of early modern Spanish scholasticism and their interpretation of Thomas Aquinas's *Summa theologiae*.[3] Although Becanus was primarily interested in the theological implications of the topic,

---

[2] Von Hagen, a doctoral candidate, is sometimes regarded as the author of the theses in light of modern academic customs—see, e.g., Richard Krebs, *Die politische Publizistik der Jesuiten und ihrer Gegner: In den letzten Jahrzehnten vor Ausbruch des Dreißigjährigen Krieges* (Halle: Niemeyer, 1890), 142; and Felix Stieve, *Die Politik Baierns 1591–1607: Zweite Hälfte* (Munich: Rieger, 1883), 919ff. But in Becanus's day, theses were usually written by the presiding professor. Furthermore, the Protestant opponents of the theses regard Becanus as the author and ignore von Hagen.

[3] Wim Decock, "Trust Beyond Faith: Re-Thinking Contracts with Heretics and Excommunicates in Times of Religious War," *Rivista Internazionale di Diritto Comune* 27 (2016): 301–28, esp. 318ff. Decock's study also provides a more in-depth account of Becanus's *De fide* in the context of early modern contract law. See also the references and footnotes in the translation of *De fide haereticis servanda* in this edition.

he showed substantial knowledge of the contemporary discussion on contract law by not only citing the sources of Roman law but also the juridical authorities such as Antonio Gómez (c. 1501–1561).[4]

The theses explicitly take on a polemical stance in response to these questions. According to Becanus himself, he not only turned against his Protestant opponents, whom he attacked on several previous occasions, but also resolutely against two specific groups of Catholic adversaries. On the one hand, he wanted to refute the "*politiques* of our time,"[5] a term often used by Jesuits and other radical anti-Machiavellists to pejoratively label jurists, politicians, and senior officials who took a pragmatic stance on confessional issues. Becanus accused the *politiques* of considering agreements and promises no longer morally obligatory if keeping them was not expedient—certainly a vast polemical exaggeration. On the other hand, Becanus repudiated a position that does not deny the moral obligation of promises but excludes contracts and promises made to heretics.

Against these two groups he repeatedly emphasized his basic principle that, according to Catholic doctrine, every agreement and promise fulfilling the requirements of moral validity[6] is morally obligatory and has to be kept as if it were made to a member of the Catholic Church.[7] Whether an agreement is between Catholics or between

---

[4] Decock, "Trust Beyond Faith," 301–28.

[5] Martinus Becanus, *Disputatio theologica, de fide haereticis servanda. Cum appendice in libellum, cui titulus: Foederatorum inferioris Germaniae defensio tertia contra calumniam pacis perturbatae &c* (Mainz, 1607), fol.)(4v: "Politicorum nostri temporis"; *On the Duty to Keep Faith with Heretics*, p. 3. This introduction cites the first edition of the work from 1607.

[6] Becanus follows the traditions of Spanish scholasticism and Roman law on the limitations of the validity of contracts. See Wim Decock, *Theologians and Contract Law: The Moral Transformation of the Ius Commune (ca. 1500–1650)* (Leiden: Brill, 2013), 215–505.

[7] Becanus, *De fide haereticis servanda*, 7.8, p. 61: "non minus, quàm Catholicis"; *On the Duty to Keep Faith with Heretics*, p. 55.

Catholics and heretics is not important for moral consideration.[8] He thoroughly substantiates this basic principle with references to canon law and the Bible—for example, to the contract between Joshua and the Gibeonites (Josh. 9:19).[9] This basic principle that Becanus develops in his theses differs—as Harro Höpfl points out—"in no way from that of any identifiable *politique*."[10] By not giving a fair representation of the *politiques*' position, Becanus masks how close his own position is to theirs. Like the *politiques* and his Catholic contemporaries in general, Becanus does not give a clear statement about a possible expiration of political agreements with heretics, such as the Peace of Augsburg.[11] He justifiably claims that his basic principle corresponds with the Catholic mainstream. Shortly after Becanus, the Antwerpian Jesuit Heribert Rosweyde (1569–1629) and the Calvinist preacher Daniel Plancius (ca. 1580–1618), from Delft, debated publicly about the issue *de fide haereticis servanda*. Plancius published his theses with that title in Latin and in Dutch, followed by homonymous books by Rosweyde

---

[8] Becanus, *De fide haereticis servanda*, 7.17, p. 67; *On the Duty to Keep Faith with Heretics*, p. 59.

[9] Becanus, *De fide haereticis servanda*, 7.9–17, pp. 61–67; *On the Duty to Keep Faith with Heretics*, pp. 55–59. Becanus derives from the Old Testament a general permission for treaties and alliances with non-Christians or non-Catholics; see Michael Becker, *Kriegsrecht im frühneuzeitlichen Protestantismus: Eine Untersuchung zum Beitrag lutherischer und reformierter Theologen, Juristen und anderer Gelehrter zur Kriegsrechtsliteratur im 16. und 17. Jahrhundert* (Tübingen: Mohr Siebeck, 2017), 287ff.

[10] Harro Höpfl, *Jesuit Political Thought: The Society of Jesus and the State, c. 1540–1630* (Cambridge: Cambridge University Press, 2004), 159.

[11] Höpfl, *Jesuit Political Thought*, 159. Many Catholic authors considered the Peace of Augsburg's validity to be in doubt since it did not include the pope and the bishops, or they considered it a transitional agreement that was suspended by the Council of Trent. See Christoph Strohm, "Konfessionsspezifische Zugänge zum Augsburger Religionsfrieden bei lutherischen, reformierten und katholischen Juristen," in *Der Augsburger Religionsfrieden 1555*, ed. Heinz Schilling and Heribert Smolinsky (Gütersloh: Gütersloher Verlagshaus, 2007), 127–56, esp. 142–54.

and his fellow Jesuit Robert Sweerts (1570–1646).[12] Rosweyde and Sweerts share Becanus's main principle: that all morally valid contracts and promises must be fulfilled. Due to the lack of explicit references, it remains unclear whether Becanus or the Dutch authors knew of each other's works.

By emphasizing that this basic principle is rooted in Catholic doctrine and is universally taught by the church, Becanus reacts to the repeated accusations of Protestants claiming otherwise. One popular historical example Protestant polemicists cited to prove their point was that Jan Hus had been executed during the Council of Constance in 1415, despite his being guaranteed safe conduct.[13] The common accusation among Protestant polemicists that Catholics did not honor their agreements and contracts with heretics was also made by the jurist Michael Loefenius (1550–1620). As a government official of the Palatinate, the leading territory of Reformed confession in the Empire, he wrote a widely acknowledged polemic against the "highly dangerous doctrine and practise of the Pope and the Jesuits," published in 1606 in Heidelberg.[14] The idea advanced by Felix Stieve, that this publication provoked the archbishop of Mainz to order a disputation *de fide*

---

[12] Daniel Plancius, *Dissertatio de fide haereticis non servanda* (Amsterdam, 1608); Daniel Plancius, *Reden-strijd van de Ketters ghenn gheloove te houden* (Amsterdam, 1609); Heribert Rosweyde, *De fide haereticis servanda* (Antwerp, 1610); and Robert Sweerts, *De fide haereticis servanda* (Antwerp, 1611).

[13] Becanus, *De fide haereticis servanda*, 12, pp. 108–23; *On the Duty to Keep Faith with Heretics*, pp. 93–103. Becanus argues that Hus was only guaranteed safe conduct in terms of protection against illegitimate prosecution. This would not have been violated by the legitimate condemnation of the council. For the Protestant use of this example, see Joseph Lecler, *Histoire de la tolérance au siècle de la réforme* (Paris: Montaigne, 1955), 1:285, 293–95; and Thomas A. Fudge, *The Trial of Jan Hus: Medieval Heresy and Criminal Procedure* (Oxford: Oxford University Press, 2013), 177–84.

[14] Michael Loefenius, *Wolmeinende Warnung An alle Christliche Potentaten und Obrigkeiten/ Wider Deß Bapsts unnd seiner Jesuiten hochgefehrliche Lehr und Prackticken* (Heidelberg, 1606).

haereticis servanda, may be highly speculative, but it is nevertheless probable that Becanus knew of this successful publication.[15]

Becanus's confrontation with his Protestant opponents did not merely contribute to his choice of the disputation's topic. The publication of the theses triggered a long-lasting interconfessional controversy. His first opponent, Cornelis van Brederode (ca. 1559–1637), the Dutch ambassador to the German princes, wrote anonymous pamphlets against Becanus, who in return replied to his adversary, defending his position. Later, Becanus exchanged polemical treatises with the Reformed theologian David Pareus (1548–1622), who attacked his stance on agreements with heretics once again. It is necessary for a comprehensive understanding of Becanus's theses *De fide haereticis servanda* to view them as embedded in this interconfessional controversy. Therefore, it will be a major point of this introduction to take the literary context of his theses into account.

Since he was overshadowed by his much-better-known contemporary and fellow Jesuit Robert Bellarmine (1542–1621), Becanus has received only occasional attention from posterity.[16] The *Disputatio theologica de fide haereticis servanda* is one of Becanus's best-known works. This rather small publication may seem, at first glance, to be a piece of occasional academic literature like many others. Yet it has been the subject of many studies, in particular on the history of tolerance in early modern Europe. It is remarkable to see the vast differences among scholars in their evaluations of Becanus's concept of toler-

---

[15] Stieve, *Die Politik Baierns*, 920.

[16] Some of his books, especially his *Manuale controversiarum huius temporis*, were republished multiple times until the late eighteenth century. There are a couple of studies that consider the life and work of Becanus within a broader context—the history of the Jesuit college of Mainz, his participation in the controversy over the Oath of Allegiance, and his position on tolerance (see below). Yet there is no comprehensive account of his work apart from the confessionalistic and methodically rather insufficient book written by Otto Happel, *Katholisches und Protestantisches Christentum nach der Auffassung der alten katholischen Polemik insbesondere des Martinus Becanus* (Würzburg: Göbel, 1898).

ance. The traditional view of Becanus considers him to be an important milestone in the history of religious toleration in early modern Europe. While scholars holding this traditional position do not deny the flaws of Becanus's concept in light of modern understanding, they do contrast him with the vast majority of his Catholic and Protestant contemporaries. This position is held not only by Becanus's fellow Jesuit scholars Bernhard Duhr (1852–1930) and Joseph Lecler (1895–1988), author of the several-times translated *Histoire de la tolérance au siècle de la Réforme*, but also by Klaus Schreiner (1931–2015).[17] Other scholars consider that Becanus has put forward "remarkably pragmatic notions"[18] on tolerance, to say the least. In contrast to this traditional view, Sascha Salatowsky argues in a recent study that Becanus's concepts were essentially identical to those of his colleague Robert Bellarmine. They should not be seen as an expression of tolerance but rather of "naked terror."[19]

Toleration, as reflected in an agreement with heretics, is merely a subordinate consideration among other applications of the general topic in *De fide haereticis servanda*. Yet apart from modern attention to the subject of toleration, Becanus's concept of toleration deserves to be another major point of this introduction. His adversaries pushed the topic in the ongoing controversy, and Becanus interestingly put his own theses into practice. As court confessor to Emperor Ferdinand II,

---

[17] See Lecler, *Histoire de la tolérance*, 1:293–95; Bernhard Duhr, *Jesuiten-Fabeln: Ein Beitrag zur Kulturgeschichte*, 4th ed. (Freiburg: Herder, 1904), 157–59, 199ff., 685; and Klaus Schreiner, "Toleranz," in *Geschichtliche Grundbegriffe*, ed. O. Brunner, W. Conze, and R. Koselleck (Stuttgart: Klett, 1990), 6:445–605, esp. 482ff.

[18] "Bemerkenswert pragmatischen Auffassungen." See Helmut Gabel, "Glaube—Individuum—Reichsrecht: Toleranzdenken im Reich von Augsburg bis Münster," in *Krieg und Kultur: Die Rezeption von Krieg und Frieden in der Niederländischen Republik und im Deutschen Reich*, ed. Horst Lademacher and Simon Groenveld (Münster: Waxmann, 1998), 157–77 (here 174).

[19] "Der nackte Terror." See Sascha Salatowsky, "Zwischen Hinrichtung und Duldung: Toleranzdebatten im konfessionellen Zeitalter, 1580–1650," *Deutsche Zeitschrift für Philosophie* 63, no. 1 (2015): 22–57 (here 28).

Becanus was in a position of political influence and responsibility. After the emperor asked his confessor for guidance on the question of whether he should grant toleration to the Lutherans in Inner Austria to ensure their loyalty in threatening times, Becanus could apply and further develop his concept.

In *De fide haereticis servanda*, Becanus takes on the question of religious toleration for the first time. His basic principle, that it is morally obligatory to fulfill all contracts and promises unless they are against divine law or in another way invalid, also applies to agreements granting religious tolerance to heretics. Becanus reflects on the question of whether the principle applies to agreements granting religious tolerance to heretics at all and, if so, under which conditions such an agreement could be valid. He quickly summarizes his position in five main points:

> On this matter the decision must be made as follows: (1) Freedom of religion is by all means forbidden and goes against divine precept. (2) Freedom of religion is destructive to the state. (3) It must not be ordered, authorized, or introduced by any prince or magistrate, but rather be impeded and overthrown by all means that are appropriate and possible, at least if that can be done conveniently. (4) However, if this cannot be done conveniently, causing great damage or evil to the state, it can be tolerated for a while. (5) If it is being tolerated in this manner and an agreement has been made, faith must be kept.[20]

---

[20] Becanus, *De fide haereticis servanda*, 10.2, pp. 88–89: "De hac re ita statuendum est. 1. Libertatem Religionis omnino esse illicitam, & diuino precepto repugnantem. 2. Reipublicae esse pernitiosam. 3. non debere praecipi, approbari aut introduci ab vllo principe aut magistratu; sed potius omnibus modis, si commodè fieri potest, impediri & profligari. 4. si autem commodè impediri non possit, nisi cum maiori damno aut malo reipublicae, aliquo tempore tolerari posse. 5. & si hoc modo toleretur, & in pactum deducatur, fidem seruandam esse"; *On the Duty to Keep Faith with Heretics*, p. 77.

Introduction

Becanus differentiates between general freedom of religion (*libertas religionis*) and temporally limited and pragmatically founded toleration. The former is entirely forbidden according to Catholic doctrine. A Catholic prince cannot legitimately grant general religious liberty and is thus not obligated to observe such an agreement against divine law. To Becanus, a prince granting general religious liberty is proof of his serious lack of interest in his subjects' salvation and is thus a sign of bad governance. He also gives plenty of historical examples to substantiate his claim that general religious liberty is destructive to society. The latter—a limited toleration of heresy—can be established by a Catholic prince. But Becanus insists on certain limitations and necessary requirements even for this extenuated form of religious liberty. The promotion of the Catholic faith as the only religion in his territory must remain the primary goal of every Catholic prince. Only if he is practically incapable of achieving this can he grant limited toleration toward subjects of different faiths to prevent a greater evil (*maius malum*) for the public, such as riots and invasions: "If, however, he cannot do this without causing too much harm to the public good, he may tolerate it as a lesser evil to avoid a greater, which would have followed otherwise."[21] With this terminology of the greater or lesser evil (*maius vel minus malum*), Becanus unites with Catholic tradition. He repeatedly refers to Augustine's writings against the Donatists, Thomas Aquinas, and the Jesuit theologians Gregory of Valencia (1549–1603) and Luis de Molina,[22] who brought forward similar arguments and terminology. Yet there are slight disparities between Becanus and his Catholic forerunners in particular on the question of toleration. In the homonymous treatise *De fide haereticis servanda*, published in 1584 in Cologne, the author Johannes Molanus (1533–1585), a theologian

---

[21] Becanus, *De fide haereticis servanda*, 10.14, p. 102: "si tamen id facere non possit sine grauiori incommodo boni publici, potest eam tolerare, tanquam minus malum, ad euitandum maius, quod alioqui sequeretur"; *On the Duty to Keep Faith with Heretics*, p. 86.

[22] See, e.g., Becanus, *De fide haereticis servanda*, 10.14, pp. 102–3; *On the Duty to Keep Faith with Heretics*, p. 86. See also the footnotes of this edition's translation.

of Louvain University, also examines the question of religious toleration, but more marginally than Becanus.[23] Molanus likewise sees an opportunity to exceptionally grant limited toleration to prevent a greater evil, yet he warns more intensely than Becanus of the possible damage and recommends consulting the pope beforehand.[24] Combining a restrictive stance on religious liberty with the possibility of pragmatic exceptions may well be called a commonplace of the Catholic political authors in Germany in the late sixteenth and early seventeenth centuries. Similar positions can be found in the work of Becanus's predecessor in Mainz, Petrus Thyraeus (1546–1601), the imperial councilor Andreas Erstenberger (d. 1592), and the Freiburg theologian Johann Paul Windeck (d. 1620).[25]

Even though he presents himself as teaching no differently from Thomas Aquinas, Becanus—like many other scholars of his time—gives something of a reinterpretation of the high scholastic authority. He adopts an influential theorem of Aquinas, using the terminology of the greater or lesser evil: "Even though the infidels sin in performing their rites, they are to be tolerated either for some good that may come

---

[23] Becanus knew of this publication and cited it. The phrase "fides haereticis servanda" was common, and Becanus does not necessarily allude to Molanus. Becanus's approach also differs from Molanus's in focusing more on juridical questions and sources.

[24] Johannes Molanus, *Libri quinque, De fide haereticis servanda tres, De fide rebellibus servanda, liber unus, qui est quartus: Item unicus, De fide et iuramento, quae a tyranno exiguntur, qui est quintus* (Cologne, 1584), 43ff. A version of this book can be found in the old library catalogue of the Jesuit college of Mainz, Stadtarchiv Mainz, signatur 14/32, https://faust.mainz.de/hzeig.FAU?sid=12650087103&dm=1&ind=1&zeig=14+/+32.

[25] Petrus Thyraeus, *De libertate fidei religionis Christianae disputatio theologica tripartita* (Mainz 1590), 21ff.; for Erstenberger and Windeck, see Bernd Christian Schneider, Ius Reformandi: *Die Entwicklung des Staatskirchenrechts von seinen Anfängen bis zum Ende des Alten Reiches* (Tübingen: Mohr Siebeck, 2001), 183; and Christoph Strohm, *Calvinismus und Recht: Weltanschaulich-konfessionelle Aspekte im Werk reformierter Juristen in der Frühen Neuzeit* (Tübingen: Mohr Siebeck, 2008), 379–89.

from it or for some evil that may be avoided."²⁶ Aquinas, however, makes a neat distinction between infidels, to whom this quote refers, and heretics, who are by no means to be tolerated.²⁷ Becanus ignores this distinction and claims that this quote refers to gentiles, infidels, and heretics together: "The rites of pagans and heretics may be tolerated to prevent a greater evil."²⁸

This observation should not distract us from Becanus's rather uncompromising stance toward heretics from a modern point of view. He endorses secular punishments for heretics, including the death penalty, though he adds that this could not be implemented in Germany.²⁹ Becanus defends this strict position against Protestant accusations by pointing to the situation in the Protestant Netherlands, where Catholics would not be granted any religious freedom.³⁰

---

²⁶ Thomas Aquinas, *Summa theologiae*, II-II, Q.10, art.11: "quamvis infideles in suis ritibus peccent, tolerari possunt vel propter aliquod bonum quod ex eis provenit, vel propter aliquod malum quod vitatur."

²⁷ See Thomas Aquinas, *Summa theologiae*, II-II, Q.11, art. 3.

²⁸ Becanus, *De fide haereticis servanda*, 10.14, pp. 102–3: "ritus gentilum & haereticorum tolerari posse, ad maius euitandum"; *On the Duty to Keep Faith with Heretics*, p. 86.

²⁹ Becanus, *De fide haereticis servanda*, 8.14–18, pp. 77–81; *On the Duty to Keep Faith with Heretics*, pp. 66–69.

³⁰ Becanus, *De fide haereticis servanda*, Appendix, prop. 5, p. 143; *On the Duty to Keep Faith with Heretics*, p. 117. For the situation of the Catholic minority in the Dutch Republic in the early seventeenth century, see Christine Kooi, "Paying Off the Sheriff: Strategies of Catholic Toleration in Golden Age Holland," in *Calvinism and Religious Toleration in the Dutch Golden Age*, ed. R. Po-Chia Hsia and Henk Van Nierop (Cambridge: Cambridge University Press, 2002), 87–101; Andrew Pettegree, "The Politics of Toleration in the Free Netherlands, 1572–1620," in *Tolerance and Intolerance in the European Reformation*, ed. Ole Peter Grell and Bob Scribner (Cambridge: Cambridge University Press, 1996), 182–98; and Christine Kooi, *Calvinists and Catholics during Holland's Golden Age: Heretics and Idolaters* (Cambridge: Cambridge University Press, 2012), 99–107.

Despite his severe point of view, Becanus displays a pragmatic position toward everyday contact with heretics. Because the Protestants of his day were not excommunicated by name, canon law provisions restricting contact with those who were excommunicated would therefore not apply.[31] As long as there was no danger to the salvation of Catholic souls, even a matrimonial contract could be concluded between a Catholic and a heretic and must be kept.[32]

The two major points of this introduction—interconfessional controversy and Becanus's concept of toleration—are closely linked. Positive remarks on Becanus by Lecler, Duhr, and other scholars primarily refer to his *Manuale controversiarum huius temporis*. In the sixteen years between his first and his final publication on toleration, Becanus further developed his concept. Controversies with his Protestant opponents and later experiences as the emperor's court confessor will be regarded as essential parts of this development.

Becanus's Controversy with Brederode

Becanus's theses *De fide haereticis servanda* were the starting point of a controversy that lasted for some years after their publication in 1607. The main reason for this does not lie in any peculiarity regarding the theses, but in Becanus's appendix to the book. This appendix attacks a small pamphlet titled *Foederatorum inferioris Germaniae defensio tertia, contra calumniam pacis perturbatae et penitus reiectae*. Published earlier in 1607, this pamphlet refers to the preliminary negotiations of the Twelve Years' Truce (*Twaalfjarig Bestand*, 1609–1621) between

---

[31] Becanus, *De fide haereticis servanda*, 8.8–11, pp. 72–75; *On the Duty to Keep Faith with Heretics*, pp. 64–66.

[32] Becanus, *De fide haereticis servanda*, 9, pp. 81–87; *On the Duty to Keep Faith with Heretics*, pp. 71–75. See Horst Dreitzel, "Toleranz und Gewissensfreiheit im konfessionellen Zeitalter: Zur Diskussion im Reich zwischen Augsburger Religionsfrieden und Aufklärung," in *Religion und Religiosität im Zeitalter des Barock*, ed. Dieter Breuer, vol. 1 (Wiesbaden: Harrassowitz, 1995), 115–28, esp. 120; and Happel, *Katholisches und Protestantisches Christentum*, 44.

INTRODUCTION

the Netherlands and Spain and is the third installment in a series of pamphlets concerning the negotiations.[33]

The author of this anonymous pamphlet is presumably Pieter Cornelis van Brederode (ca. 1559–1637), the Dutch ambassador to the German princely courts.[34] An emphasis of Brederode's service was to promote Dutch interests in Protestant territories and especially in the Palatinate, as the leading territory of Reformed confession in the Empire, and to gather financial aid for the war against Spain. He wrote several printed as well as handwritten pamphlets, which he sent to the courts in the Empire.[35] Brederode promoted the uncompromising position of the Dutch, who tried to make use of their recent naval victories in the negotiations. Hence, he tried to convince the German allies in this very costly war of the necessity of not rushing into a possibly unfavorable peace treaty. He accused the Spanish of not being obligated to honor a treaty with heretics because of their Catholic faith. As the Spanish were even more fraudulent than the Turks, a generic peace treaty with the tyrannical Philipp III of Spain seemed impossible.[36] Brederode referred to a collection of quotes derived from canon law, papal documents, and Jesuit authors. The question of religious tolerance was a bitterly disputed issue during

---

[33] It was preceded by the pseudonymous Francus Germanus, *Repraesentatio pacis generalis* (s.l., 1607); and the anonymous *Foederatorum inferioris Germaniae defensio secunda* (s.l., s.a.). See Uwe Sibeth, "Der 'Friede' als Fortsetzung des Krieges mit anderen Mitteln: Zur Representatio pacis generalis (1607) des Pieter Cornelisz Brederode," in *Wege der Neuzeit: Festschrift für Heinz Schilling zum 65. Geburtstag*, ed. Stefan Ehrenpreis et al. (Berlin: Duncker und Humblot, 2007), 479–84.

[34] Sibeth, "Friede als Fortsetzung," 484ff.

[35] Sibeth, "Friede als Fortsetzung," 485; for Brederode's activity in Germany, see Johannes Arndt, *Das Heilige Römische Reich und die Niederlande 1566 bis 1648: Politisch-konfessionelle Verflechtung und Publizistik im Achtzigjährigen Krieg* (Cologne: Böhlau, 1998), 82.

[36] [Pieter Cornelis van Brederode], *Foederatorum inferioris Germaniae defensio tertia, contra calumniam pacis perturbatae et penitus reiectae* (s.l., 1607), 59–67.

xxi

the negotiations for the truce. The Spanish demanded tolerance for all Catholics in the Dutch Republic without offering reciprocal toleration for Protestants in the Spanish Netherlands.[37]

Being a Catholic Dutchman himself, Martinus Becanus (van der Beeck) was provoked by Brederode's pamphlet to refute it. In his appendix he gives a short apologetic summary of his theses focused on Brederode's accusations. Brederode responded with another anonymous pamphlet titled *Pro defensione tertia foederatum* in 1608. He generally refutes Becanus's argumentation and tries to demonstrate his disingenuousness. Brederode interprets Becanus's remark on the Dutch Republic not granting religious freedom to Catholics as a confession of not intending to keep any contract concerning toleration. He defends the Dutch practice of suppressing Catholicism as a necessary means to prevent the Spanish Inquisition from spreading into the republic. Brederode is nevertheless convinced of the moral superiority of the Dutch Protestants, who would not extirpate people of a different faith as did the Catholics all over Europe.[38]

Becanus, who was not yet aware that Brederode was his opponent, met the Dutch ambassador in person in summer 1608 on a trip to the hot springs at Schwalbach. Brederode, though not revealing himself as Becanus's opponent, publicly mocked him on this occasion.[39] The

---

[37] Werner Thomas, "The Treaty of London, the Twelve Years Truce and Religious Toleration in Spain and the Netherlands," in *The Twelve Years Truce (1609): Peace, Truce, War and Law in the Low Countries at the Turn of the 17th Century*, ed. Randall Lesaffer (Leiden: Brill, 2014), 277–97, esp. 288; and Alicia Esteban Estríngana, "Preparing the Ground: The Cession of the Netherlands' Sovereignty in 1598 and the Failure of Its Peace-Making Objective (1607–1609)," in Lesaffer, ed., *Twelve Years Truce (1609)*, 15–47, esp. 38–47.

[38] [Pieter Cornelis van Brederode], *Pro defensione tertia foederatum contra Appendicem Disputationis Theologicae, De Fide Haereticis servanda, Martini Becani* (Amsterdam, 1608), 74: "non extirpantur, vti in Italia, Hispania, Austria, & alibi Euangelici."

[39] Martinus Becanus, *Epistola Martini Becani Societatis Jesu theologi ad D. Davidem Pareum* (Mainz, 1619), 51; for the meeting in Schwalbach, see

Jesuit continued to defend his case against his unknown Dutch opponent in 1609 under the title *Quaestiones miscellaneae de fide haereticis servanda: Contra quendam Calvinistam Batavum, qui se foederatorum inferioris Germaniae defensorem appellat*. In this book Becanus does not take on the issue of tolerance and religious freedom. Instead, he focuses on the underlying question: Which church truly is to be called catholic? In doing so, Becanus tries to disprove Brederode's argument that Reformed Protestantism is the true catholic church. In the last chapter of the book, Becanus tries once again to show that his basic rule is taught by the whole Catholic Church, citing theological authorities and canon law.

In 1610 Brederode responded with another anonymous pamphlet titled *Apologia pro Christiano Batavo, non Calvinista, contra Martini Becani Jesuitae, antichristiani sylvaducensis quaestiones miscellaneas; De fide haereticis servanda*. It was published in Hanau near Frankfurt, Brederode's residence at the time, though the imprint gives London as the place of publication.[40] Brederode presumably wanted to give the impression that another Protestant author was coming to his defense, a technique sometimes used by controversialists of those days. The *Apologia pro Christiano Batavo* is more extensive by far than his previous publications and includes several historical examples and documents in order to prove the unreliability and the fraudulent

---

David Pareus, *Acta Colloquiorum Swalbacensium* (Heidelberg, 1618), 12ff.; Tobias Dienst, "Das 'Schwalbacher Kolloquium' 1608 und sein publizistisches Nachspiel: Mündliche und schriftliche interkonfessionelle Kommunikation vor dem Dreißigjährigen Krieg," in *Jahrbuch der Hessischen Kirchengeschichtlichen Vereinigung* 68 (2017): 201–35.

[40] The imprint *Londini* can be found in many publications printed in Hanau during that time. The imprint *Hanau* can be found in some old library catalogues like the one of Heidelberg University. The assumption made by the *Verzeichnis der im deutschen Sprachraum erschienenen Drucke des 17. Jahrhunderts* (www.vd17.de) that this was a work of the English theologian Matthew Sutcliffe (d. 1629), who encountered Becanus in the controversy about the Oath of Allegiance, is implausible. See the catalog record for item number 23:272917B, http://gso.gbv.de/DB=1.28/CMD?ACT=SRCHA&IKT =8002&TRM=%2723:272917B%27.

conduct of Catholics toward people of different faiths. He also returns to the issue of tolerance and religious freedom. Brederode insists that Catholics had always broken their commitments and agreements in this regard.[41] Contrary to Becanus's explicit basic principle, Brederode tries to establish a different general rule of the Catholics: "In the case of the free exercise of religion, faith is either not to be granted to heretics, or—if granted—not to be kept."[42]

These renewed accusations gave rise to another reply from Becanus. The *Quaestiones Batavicae in quendam Batavum, qui se Christianum, evangelicum, & foederatorum defensorem appellat* were published in 1611 and match Brederode's *Apologia pro Christiano Batavo* in terms of sheer extent. Again Becanus omits the issue of tolerance for the most part and dedicates a large amount of his argumentation to another topic. In 1610 King Henry IV of France was killed by an assassin with alleged ties to the Jesuits. Because of Brederode's remarks on this occasion and on the Spanish Jesuit Juan de Mariana's theses on tyrannicide,[43] Becanus was eager to defend his order. Following the official position of the Society of Jesus, Becanus denied any proximity of the Jesuits and the Catholic Church to regicide and extensively rejected the accusations.[44] After this publication, the controversy between Becanus and the Dutch ambassador ended.

---

[41] [Pieter Cornelis van Brederode], *Apologia pro Christiano Batavo, non Calvinista, contra Martini Becani Jesuitae, antichristiani sylvaducensis quaestiones miscellaneas; De fide haereticis servanda* (London [Hanau], 1610), 212ff.

[42] [Brederode], *Apologia pro Christiano Batavo*, 251: "Regulam ... Generalem"; "Fidem Haereticis vel non dandam, vel datam non esse seruandam, si illis data sit super libero Religionis suae exercitio."

[43] See Harald Braun, *Juan de Mariana and Early Modern Spanish Political Thought* (Aldershot: Ashgate, 2011); Höpfl, *Jesuit Political Thought*, 314–38.

[44] Martinus Becanus, *Quaestiones Batavicae in quendam Batavum, qui se Christianum, evangelicum, & foederatorum defensorem appellat* (Mainz, 1611), esp. 42–44.

Becanus's Controversy with Pareus

Although the controversy between Becanus and Brederode came to a halt, the issues of contractual faithfulness and tolerance continued to be a matter of public interest. In 1616 two vernacular pamphlets were published in the Empire to present the issue to a broader audience. The Catholic convert, scholar, and controversialist Caspar Schoppe (1576–1649) pseudonymously published a polemical pamphlet[45] in which he explicitly praised the "excellent and most famous" theses of Becanus.[46] In the same year another book that considered the issue was published on behalf of the Protestants. The dialogue *Ein Catholisch Tisch-Gespräch*[47] is a fictional conversation between different Protestant and Catholic characters about keeping faith with heretics. While obviously written by a Protestant, it differentiates between "good" Catholics with a naive or pragmatic political stance, and "bad" Catholics—namely, the Jesuits, who permit perjury and the breaking of contracts with heretics. This pamphlet was reprinted several times until 1655.[48] It is part of a vast amount of anti-Jesuit literature that became a genre of its own in early modern Europe

---

[45] Christoph von Ungersdorff [Caspar Schoppe], *Erinnerung von der Calvinisten falschen betrüglichen Art und Feindseligkeit gegen dem heiligen Römischen Reich. Item/ Widerholung der Catholischen Scribenten/ sonderlich der Herrn Jesuiter Lehr und Meynung vom Religions Frieden/ und ob Ketzern/ Trew und Glaub zu halten sey* (s.l., 1616). As a young Protestant scholar, Schoppe was respected for his philological studies. After he converted to Catholicism and emigrated to Rome, he established himself as a well-known polemical writer.

[46] Ungersdorff [Schoppe], *Erinnerung von der Calvinisten*, 84: "fürtreffliche[n] hochberümbte[n]."

[47] A. I. F. [Johann Fadenrecht, pseud.], *Ein Catholisch Tisch-Gespräch. Eines Alten Teutschen/ Jungen Studenten/ Gemeinen Priesters/ und Verrufften uberwitzigen Jesuiters. Von der disputirlichen Frage: Ob man schuldig/ einem jeden/ Trew und Glauben/ Eyd und Verheis zu halten* (s.l., 1616).

[48] There are two sequels to this book pseudonymously ascribed to the names Lügenfeindt and Huldreich.

INTRODUCTION

and that was even adapted in the Catholic parts of the Continent.[49] A common accusation in these pamphlets claims that the Society of Jesus would allow its members to lie for their own advantage by using sly equivocations. The Jesuits in particular were accused of lying to heretics and not keeping faith with them.

In 1618 the Reformed theologian David Pareus (1548–1622) carried on the controversy with Becanus. He was a professor in Heidelberg and one of the most renowned Reformed theologians of his day.[50] He was present in 1608 when Becanus and Brederode met at the hot springs at Schwalbach, where he staged a spontaneous colloquium with his archrival Becanus, with whom he had gotten into a couple of controversies earlier. Pareus presumably was in contact with Brederode, who (like himself) lived in Heidelberg, the capital of the Palatinate, between 1610 and 1621. The Palatinate was one of the most important allies of the Dutch and supported the Republic politically and with financial and military aid.[51] Dutch and Heidelberg scholars, associated by their shared Reformed confession, corresponded with one another.

Pareus delivered and afterward published a speech titled *Oratio inauguralis de fide haereticis servanda: Num serio sic sentiant Iesuitae*

---

[49] Ursula Paintner, '*Des Papsts neue Creatur*': *Antijesuitische Publizistik im Deutschsprachigen Raum, 1555–1618* (Amsterdam: Rodopi, 2011); and Pierre-Antoine Fabre and Catherine Maire, eds., *Les antijésuites: Discours, figures et lieux de l'antijésuitisme à l'époque modern* (Rennes: Presses Universitaires, 2010).

[50] David Pareus attracted students from all over Europe to Heidelberg. As a recognized theological authority among Reformed scholars, Pareus wrote a letter to the Synod of Dordt (he could not attend) that was read and discussed in two sessions. He is best known for his conmmentary on the epistle to the Romans and his attempt to establish an irenic union between European Protestants. See Howard Hotson, "Irenicism in the Confessional Age: The Holy Roman Empire, 1563–1648," in *Conciliation and Confession: The Struggle for Unity in the Age of Reform, 1415–1648*, ed. Howard Louthan and Randall C. Zachman (Notre Dame, IN: Notre Dame University Press, 2004), 228–85, esp. 233–45.

[51] See Arndt, *Das Heilige Römische Reich*, 169–75.

& Sophistae in Papatu, in which he attacks Becanus and other Catholic authors. Alluding to common anti-Jesuit sentiments, Pareus accuses his opponent of being duplicitous in his theses. He considers his opponent's basic rule that all agreements must be observed, even if concluded with heretics, as being "fine words, but double-tongued, of a conspiratorial and perfidious mind."[52] Like Brederode, Pareus focuses on the issue of toleration to prove Becanus's theses to be self-contradictory sophisms. On the one hand, Becanus would exclude the possibility of religious freedom, calling it "plainly forbidden"; on the other hand, he would call it "licit and honorable"[53] as an exception to prevent a greater evil. This pragmatic stance toward tolerance is nothing more than a "sly disguise of perfidy"[54] to Pareus. The ground of such an agreement was not truthfulness, justice, or fidelity, but rather the "interests of the Papists, or their fear."[55] This would be a horrific concept for the Protestants since they could not rely on agreements of uncertain duration. The Catholic party could break the agreement in a situation of strength, when a greater evil was no longer to be expected. Pareus also relates this to the Peace of Augsburg, which he considers to be a "treaty … about religious liberty in the Empire."[56] Like many Protestants, especially in the Palatinate, Pareus believes the Peace of Augsburg is in grave danger.[57]

Pareus himself was far from promoting universal religious tolerance. Christian princes and authorities were obliged to enforce the true religion with infidels and blasphemers, due to their duties according to

---

[52] David Pareus, *Oratio inauguralis de fide haereticis servanda* (Heidelberg, 1618), 6: "Bona verba: Estis hic lingua diuisi: mente conspiratis in perfidia."

[53] Pareus, *Oratio inauguralis*, 9; see Becanus, *De fide haereticis servanda*, 10.3, p. 89 ("planè illicita"); 10.16, p. 104 ("licitum & honestum"); *On the Duty to Keep Faith with Heretics*, p. 78, p. 87.

[54] Pareus, *Oratio inauguralis*, 8: "vafrum perfidiae tegumentum."

[55] Pareus, *Oratio inauguralis*, 8: "vtilitas Pontificiorum, vel metus."

[56] Pareus, *Oratio inauguralis*, 7: "Pactum habent Pontificii & Euangelici de libertate Religionis Euangelicae in Imperio."

[57] See Strohm, "Konfessionsspezifische Zugänge zum Augsburger," 142–54.

Romans 13:4.[58] Pareus leaves open whether only anti-Trinitarians and other fringe groups are included in this, or Catholics are as well. In his widely read commentary on the epistle to the Romans, Pareus refers to the example of the kings of the Old Testament such as Hezekiah and Josiah, who enforced religious reforms. Regarding "idolatry," a term Pareus uses for clandestine Catholic worship in Protestant territories, he coins the phrase "Do not tolerate, but abolish it" (*non tolerare, sed tollere*).[59]

Meanwhile, teaching at the University of Vienna, Becanus responded to Pareus in an open letter published in 1619.[60] He accuses Pareus of purposefully misunderstanding him. Trying to avoid a greater evil was not a sign of perfidy but a requirement of nature, and Pareus would be insane if he thought otherwise.[61] Nevertheless, Becanus shows a remarkable flexibility in his argument. A main topic of his controversy with Brederode was whether Catholics or Protestants are truly to be called heretics. Here Becanus is willing to put this question aside. He then reformulates his basic principle even toward the undisputed heretics of early Christianity: "Promises, agreements, and bargains are to be served toward Manichaeans and Donatists."[62] On the contrary, those who make oaths and contracts that break divine law, including religious tolerance, are not obliged to fulfill them without a compelling cause. Becanus illustrates this with a rather distasteful fictional example of Pareus making an adulterous contract with another woman

---

[58] Pareus, *Oratio inauguralis*, 9ff.; Rom. 13:4: "For he [the authority] is God's servant for your good. But if you do wrong, be afraid, for he does not bear the sword in vain. For he is the servant of God, an avenger who carries out God's wrath on the wrongdoer."

[59] David Pareus, *In divinam ad Romanos epistolam commentarius* (Heidelberg, 1608), 1401.

[60] In the meantime, Becanus learned that Brederode was his earlier opponent: Becanus, *Epistola*, 51.

[61] Becanus, *Epistola*, 74.

[62] Becanus, *Epistola*, 64: "In Promissis, pactis, & conuentis, seruanda est fides Manichaeis & Donatistis."

to poison his wife. No legal expert, not even a Protestant one, would declare such a morally repellent contract to be mandatory.[63]

Furthermore, Becanus clarifies an important point of his argument in response to accusations that he is "double-tongued." Unlike the common practice of his time,[64] Becanus explicitly distinguishes between the terms "freedom of religion" (*libertas religionis*) and "toleration" (*tolerantia*)—a distinction he implicitly brought up in his earlier works:

> The one thing is freedom of religion, or the free exercise of a heretic religion; the other thing is toleration of this exercise. Free exercise of a heretic religion is always illicit. No agreements can be made about it. But toleration of this exercise can be licit and can therefore be the subject of an agreement.[65]

In the controversy with Pareus, Becanus is compelled by his Protestant opponent to engage in the subject of agreements with heretics again. Due to Pareus's accusations, he clarifies and further develops his argument especially concerning religious toleration.

Becanus's Controversy with His Roman Superiors

In early 1620 Becanus was appointed court confessor of Emperor Ferdinand II, a position that entailed a certain amount of political influence at the court. He took this office in a crucial moment of the Habsburg monarchy. In the course of the Bohemian Revolt, some

---

[63] Becanus, *Epistola*, 68, 77. In the scholastic tradition, contracts for sex and murder are common examples of the limitations of morally valid contracts. In the given case, an immoral act is the object of the contract (*causa materialis*) and is therefore void. See Wim Decock, *Theologians and Contract Law*, 420–25.

[64] See Schreiner, "Toleranz," 495.

[65] Becanus, *Epistola*, 81: "Aliud est, libertas religionis, seu liberum exercitium haereticae religionis; aliud tolerantia illius exercitij: Liberum exercitium haereticae religionis semper est illicitum, & de eo pacisci non licet. At tolerantia illius exercitij potest esse licita, ac proinde de tolerantia licitè pacisci quis potest."

Austrian estates had joined the confederation against Ferdinand, who relied heavily on the military help of Maximilian of Bavaria and the Spanish troops. In this situation, the emperor considered settling the claims of the Lutheran estates in Inner Austria for toleration of the Augsburg Confession and asked his new confessor Becanus for guidance.[66] To Becanus, the threat of invasion by Frederick V's (the "Winter King's") Bohemian and Palatinate troops and the risk of an expanding revolt in the Austrian mainland was a model example of a "greater evil." Therefore, he recommended granting temporally and locally limited toleration of religious worship to the Lutherans.[67]

Emperor Ferdinand and his Jesuit confessor were not able to convince the pope and the superior general of the Society of Jesus of their initiative, yet they persisted with their plans. This put Becanus in the position of having to defend himself to Rome. He sent apologetic letters to his admired friend Robert Bellarmine, the cardinal and most influential Catholic controversialist. Becanus's relationship with Rome was already very strained. In a controversy with Anglican theologians about King James I's Oath of Allegiance, carried out between 1609 and 1613, Becanus became internationally prominent as an uncompromising polemical author. Yet he crossed a line by implying that the pope had the right to have a tyrannical king killed.[68] In an unsuccessful attempt

---

[66] Arno Strohmeyer, *Konfessionskonflikt und Herrschaftsordnung: Widerstandsrecht bei den österreichischen Ständen (1550–1650)* (Mainz: Philipp von Zabern, 2006), 199–341, esp. 266.

[67] Bernhard Duhr, *Geschichte der Jesuiten in den Ländern deutscher Zunge*, vol. 2, pt. 2 (Freiburg: Herder, 1913), 220–22; Lecler, *Histoire de la tolérance*, 1:295; and Dreitzel, *Toleranz und Gewissensfreiheit*, 120.

[68] Martinus Becanus, *Controversia Anglicana: De potestate Regis et Pontificis* (Mainz, 1612), 123ff. Becanus does not explicitly promote the pope's right to have a king killed, but he interprets the execution of Queen Athaliah (2 Kings 11), ordered by the high priest Jehoiada, as a model for the pope's temporal power. The outrage over Becanus's theses in France and England was also because of his comments that Athaliah was the rightful queen since she had the people's approval even though she did not have a birthright to the throne of Judah. Becanus, *Controversia Anglicana*, 120ff.

to prevent a condemnation by the infuriated Sorbonne University in Paris, the Vatican placed Becanus's book *Controversia Anglicana* on the *Index Librorum Prohibitorum*.[69] Even though Becanus was given the chance to emend his work in a second edition, leading to the removal of his book from the Index, he was from then on under constant observation by the order's generalate.

In the case of the Austrian Lutherans, Becanus rejected Bellarmine's recommendation to make an ambiguous offer that would not explicitly grant toleration and that would be open for interpretation. In this instance, Becanus proved his independence from Bellarmine.[70] To him, such an offer would add grist to the mills of his Protestant opponents, who accused the Catholics of being "double-tongued." Becanus defended the emperor's toleration plans as sufficiently limited, since they were aimed only at the "more peace-minded"[71] Lutherans, excluding the Calvinists. The terms of toleration were comparable to the policy regarding the Jews in the Papal States. In a report sent to the Jesuit headquarters in Rome, Becanus emphasized the necessity of limited toleration, alluding to the terminology of Thomas Aquinas. Unlike his former approaches to the issue, Becanus was no longer limiting toleration to prevent greater evil. He also accepted it to achieve a "greater good" (*maius bonum*)—a term he did not use in his previous writings. In this specific case, a military alliance with Saxony was expected, and Becanus expressed his hopes for the future conversion of many Austrian Lutherans if they would be treated indulgently.[72] This is a significant change in his concept of tolerance. It is a first step

---

[69] Tutino, *Empire of Souls*, 211–61.

[70] Salatowsky, "Zwischen Hinrichtung und Duldung," 30ff., considers Becanus's and Bellarmine's concepts as being one and the same ("ein und dieselbe").

[71] Becanus to Bellarmine, August 8, 1620, in *Geschichte der a Moralstreitigkeiten in der römisch-catholischen Kirche*, ed. Ignaz von Döllinger and Franz Heinrich Reusch, vol. 2 (Nördlingen: Beck, 1889), 266: "magis pacifici."

[72] Martinus Becanus, "Casus super permissionem Imperatoris factum Austriacis Lutheranis," Archivum Romanum Societatis Iesu, Boh. 94, 80r–88v (here 86v): "etiam sperare potest multorum conversionem."

toward the idea of tolerance as possibly beneficial to society and not merely as an unpreventable nuisance and the lesser evil.

The reception of Becanus's concept of tolerance is primarily based on his late main work *Manuale controversiarum huius temporis*. It was first published in 1623 and became one of the most influential books of Catholic polemical literature, reprinted more than three dozen times all over Europe until 1771. It is a one-volume handbook of controversial theology intended as a daily tool for clergymen looking for a more easily accessible work than Bellarmine's lengthy volumes on the same subject. In his *Manuale*, Becanus relies heavily on his earlier works, which he treats as model controversies. In the passage about agreements with heretics and toleration, Becanus even directly addresses his former opponent Brederode as "Batavus"[73] and explains the situation in Austria in 1620.[74] Continuing his earlier considerations, Becanus strictly differentiates between *libertas religionis* and *tolerantia* and presents three cases in which limited toleration can be granted: "I conclude from this, that a Catholic prince can permit and tolerate heresy in his territory in three cases: First, if he cannot prevent it. Second, if by permitting it a greater good can be hoped for. Third, if a greater evil, that he cannot avert otherwise, can be prevented by permitting it."[75] The hope for a greater good (*maius bonum*), first established in the unpublished report to the generalate in 1620, is now of equal status with the bare inevitability and prevention of a greater evil. The term *maius bonum* is like its counterpart *maius malum*, adopted from Thomas Aquinas, who strictly limited this idea to the toleration of infidels—especially Jews—and explicitly excluded heretics from this

---

[73] See Martinus Becanus, *Manuale controversiarum huius temporis* (Würzburg, 1623), 5.15, pp. 711–14.

[74] Becanus, *Manuale controversiarum huius temporis*, 5.16, p. 715.

[75] Becanus, *Manuale controversiarum huius temporis*, 5.16, [p. 719] (mistakenly paginated as 717): "Ex dictis concludo, Principem Catholicum in tribus casibus posse permittere seu tolerare haeresim in sua ciuitate vel prouincia: Primò, quando non potest impedire. Secundò, quando ex permissione speratur maius bonum. Tertiò, quando ex permissione euitatur maius malum, quod aliter euitari non potest."

possibility in his *Summa* (II-II, Q. 10, art. 11). On this basis Becanus refers to the tolerated Jewish cult practices such as circumcision and Passover, which could serve as an analogy for Christian traditions like baptism and the feast of Easter.[76] But Becanus recognizes in the confessional divide of his time circumstances to be classified as a *maius bonum* too:

> If a Catholic prince could oppress the heretics by force but is convinced that a meeker approach is better [he is allowed to grant toleration] on two grounds—first, because he sees that the Catholics who live among the heretics, through a kind of pious competition, become more eager in their faith and religious practice from day to day; and that they do not only make progress in their morals and the observance of divine mandates, but that they are even encouraged to explain and defend our doctrine. Second, because he sees that they are kindled by the fervor of their Catholic neighbors and start to join them. These goods would not happen if he did not want to tolerate them.[77]

It is worth noting that Becanus emphasizes that his model Catholic prince is in fact capable of oppressing his heretic subjects. This makes the *maius bonum* an independent reason for tolerance and thus more than a supplementary justification of an inevitable necessity. His hope of a future conversion of heretics resembles Thomas Aquinas's hope that the toleration of Jews would result in similar consequences.

---

[76] Becanus, *Manuale controversiarum huius temporis*, 5.16, p. 717.

[77] Becanus, *Manuale controversiarum huius temporis*, 5.16, [p. 719] (mistakenly paginated as 717): "si Princeps Catholicus posset quidem vi coercere haereticos, sed tamen putet mitius agendum esse, ex duplici capite. Primò, quia videt Catholicos, qui viuunt inter haereticos, ex pia quadam aemulatione fieri quotidie feruentiores in sua fide ac religione; & non solum in moribus & obseruatione mandatorum Dei proficere, sed etiam magis ac magis ad doctrinam fidei nostrae explicandam & propugnandam excitari. Secundò, aduertit etiam ipsos haereticos, ex illo Catholicorum feruore paulatim accendi, & Catholicis aggregari. Haec bona non euenirent, si nollet illos tolerare."

Introduction

Becanus's other expectations set him recognizably apart from many of his Catholic contemporaries. He even attributes positive aspects to the multiconfessional communities in Germany. Instead of referring to heresy solely as a contagious disease that could spread into the Catholic population, Becanus speaks of a pious competition (*pia aemulatio*) of the confessions.

This is, however, not only a sign of his confidence in Catholic pastoral work and education but a hint about the limitations of his concept. Becanus's intention is rather a softer and hence more pragmatic take on a policy leading to religious uniformity in the form of a controlled competition rather than a promotion of "free market principles" in the religious sphere. He does not plan to permit public sermons and education of heretics. Furthermore, Becanus vehemently rejects certain reasons for toleration as illicit:

> Therefore those [princes] sin the worst who either by sheer negligence permit those [heretics] to gradually creep in; or who voluntarily tolerate [them] in the hope of worldly profit, as it is common practice in certain big trade cities, where heretics, Turks, and Moors are tolerated due to commercial interest.[78]

Becanus's critique aims at big commercial powers like the Republic of Venice and at certain concepts of toleration driven by political and economic motives. These concepts became common around 1600 and visibly replaced philosophical and theological reasons that were common in particular with the early humanists like Erasmus.[79]

---

[78] Becanus, *Manuale controversiarum huius temporis*, 5.16, [p. 719] (mistakenly paginated as 717): "Itaque peccant illi grauissimè, qui ex mera negligentia permittunt illos sensim irrepere; vel qui spè lucri témporalis, libenter eos tolerant, vt fieri solet in quibusdam magnis emporiis, vbi & haeretici, & Turcae, & Mauri tolerantur, ratione mercaturae."

[79] Hans R. Guggisberg, "Wandel der Argumente für religiöse Toleranz und Glaubensfreiheit im 16. und 17. Jahrhundert," in *Zur Geschichte der Toleranz und Religionsfreiheit*, ed. Heinrich Lutz (Darmstadt: WBG, 1977), 455–81. An early example of a concept of toleration driven by economic and political motives is the *Brief discours envoyé au roy Philippe* by the Reformed theolo-

A Milestone in the History of Tolerance?

Becanus's perspective on toleration developed over the course of sixteen years. His complete concept of tolerance, including legitimizing it as a means of promoting a greater good, which is praised by some scholars, was first published in his late work *Manuale controversiarum huius temporis* in 1623. We can see two driving forces in his development: one consists of the need to address the repeated accusations by Protestant controversialists. Becanus's main impetus to publish and publicly defend his theses is provoked by his Protestant critics, who accused the Catholics of not keeping any contracts made with heretics and being untrustworthy regarding religious toleration. In this situation of confessional competition, Becanus tried to present the Catholic side at its best to his readers in both confessional groups. The interconfessional exchange with Brederode and Pareus left its mark on the Jesuit's argumentation. He clarified his position and became more careful in his terminology concerning freedom of religion and toleration.

The other driving force behind Becanus's conceptual development seems to be his experiences as the emperor's court confessor in Vienna. Being relied on for spiritual advice, which often had grave political implications, Becanus took an even more pragmatic stance toward toleration. In his new position, Becanus gave more weight to the prince's competence in granting toleration. In his confrontation with Bellarmine and the Roman leadership of the Society of Jesus, Becanus brought forward the most important innovation in his concept of toleration: in regarding a greater good—such as the possibility of conversions—as a legitimation of religious tolerance, he noticeably departed from his former position and that of many of his contemporaries. Although being far from regarding tolerance as valuable in itself, he no longer saw it as something inherently and exclusively evil.

---

gian Franciscus Junius (Antwerp, 1566), 29ff.; see Cornel Zwierlein, *Discorso und Lex Dei: Die Entstehung neuer Denkrahmen im 16. Jahrhundert und die Wahrnehmung der französischen Religionskriege in Italien und Deutschland* (Göttingen: Vandenhoeck & Ruprecht, 2006), 385.

This development in his concept may be a reason for the vast differences in the scholarly debate. A critical appraisal of Becanus's concept of toleration depends not only on the question of whether the early or late Becanus is to be examined but also on the question of which bar is set for the evaluation of his concept of toleration. A suitable model is proposed by the German political theorist Rainer Forst in his book *Toleration in Conflict*. He distinguishes among four types of tolerance:[80] (1) the "permission conception"—the toleration of a minority by a dominant authority for pragmatic reasons; (2) the "coexistence conception," which requires a balance of rights and power; (3) the "respect conception"; and (4) the "esteem conception." The latter two conceptions are determined by a moral foundation of toleration as valuable in itself. Becanus's concept—like most other early modern models—can be portrayed as an elaborate form of the "permission conception." Hence, it does not fulfill all modern requirements for "real tolerance."

Becanus's case demonstrates the difficulties of evaluating early modern conceptions within the history of toleration. A majority of scholars regard early modern Europe as a standstill or even a setback in the historical development of tolerance.[81] Many discussions of this topic even skip the time between Sebastian Castellio and the early Enlightenment altogether.[82] In contrast to the larger-scaled concepts of many humanists or outstanding examples such as Castellio, the concepts of tolerance of Becanus and other confessionalists seem rather unimposing. The contribution of confessionalism to the history of tolerance appears to be as a negative foil that required rules in order to prevent blind fundamentalism and religiously motivated violence that

---

[80] Rainer Forst, *Toleration in Conflict: Past and Present*, trans. Ciaran Cronin (Cambridge: Cambridge University Press, 2013), 26–32.

[81] Among others, Schreiner, "Toleranz," 529ff.; and Gabel, "Glaube—Individuum—Reichsrecht," 172.

[82] For this see Salatowsky, "Zwischen Hinrichtung und Duldung," 23, who gives various examples from research literature.

could lead to civil wars.[83] This idea may have a certain explanatory potential, yet there is need to examine the confessionalists' concepts of toleration, too. Becanus provides an exceptionally extensive example of a concept of tolerance *within* a confessionalist state.[84]

Here, Becanus's concept of toleration should be understood in the context of his broader principle on agreements with heretics in all legal aspects—political, mercantile, or private. Becanus wanted to adjust the Catholic doctrine on such agreements to the requirements of his day. He and many of his Catholic contemporaries realized that it was not practical to uphold a traditional view that denied heretics certain rights in contract law—even from a confessionalist's point of view. Under pressure from the ongoing confessional divide, these Catholic canon lawyers and theologians reinterpreted their legal sources and established a "transconfessional doctrine of contract."[85] In his theses *De fide haereticis servanda* and in the ongoing controversy, Becanus promoted this reinterpretation through continuous interaction with Protestants and their allegations. The outcome is a remarkable concept of coexisting with heretics and of toleration in particular.

---

[83] A critical analysis of this concept is provided in Perez Zagorin, *How the Idea of Religious Toleration Came to the West* (Princeton, NJ: Princeton University Press, 2003), 8–13; see also Benjamin Kaplan, *Divided by Faith: Religious Conflict and the Practice of Toleration in Early Modern Europe* (Cambridge, MA: Belknap Press, 2007), 333–58.

[84] As such, Becanus's work remained an important reference for moderate Catholic politicians and the court of Vienna for decades. See Robert von Friedeburg and Michael Seidler, "The Holy Roman Empire of the German Nation," in *European Political Thought 1450–1700: Religion, Law and Philosophy*, ed. Howell A. Lloyd, Glenn Burgess, and Simon Hodson (New Haven, CT: Yale University Press, 2007), 102–75, esp. 142ff.; and Duhr, *Geschichte der Jesuiten*, 2:2:222.

[85] Decock, "Trust Beyond Faith," 328.

Introduction

Literature

Primary Sources

A. I. F. [Johann Fadenrecht, pseud.]. *Ein Catholisch Tisch-Gespräch. Eines Alten Teutschen/ Jungen Studenten/ Gemeinen Priesters/ und Verrufften uberwitzigen Jesuiters. Von der disputirlichen Frage: Ob man schuldig/ einem jeden/ Trew und Glauben/ Eyd und Verheis zu halten.* s.l., 1616.

Anonymous. *Foederatorum inferioris Germaniae defensio secunda.* s.l., s.a.

Becanus, Martinus. "Casus super permissionem Imperatoris factum Austriacis Lutheranis." Archivum Romanum Societatis Iesu, Bohemia 94, 80r–88v.

———. *Controversia Anglicana: De potestate Regis et Pontificis.* Mainz, 1612.

———. *Disputatio theologica, de fide haereticis servanda. Cum appendice in libellum, cui titulus: Foederatorum inferioris Germaniae defensio tertia contra calumniam pacis perturbatae &c.* Mainz, 1607.

———. *Epistola Martini Becani Societatis Jesu theologi ad D. Davidem Pareum.* Mainz, 1619.

———. *Manuale controversiarum huius temporis.* Würzburg, 1623.

———. *Quaestiones Batavicae in quendam Batavum, qui se Christianum, evangelicum, & foederatorum defensorem appellat.* Mainz, 1611.

[Brederode, Pieter Cornelis van]. *Apologia pro Christiano Batavo, non Calvinista, contra Martini Becani Jesuitae, antichristiani sylvaducensis quaestiones miscellaneas; De fide haereticis servanda.* London [Hanau], 1610.

———. *Foederatorum inferioris Germaniae defensio tertia, contra calumniam pacis perturbatae et penitus reiectae.* s.l., 1607.

———. *Pro defensione tertia foederatum contra Appendicem Disputationis Theologicae, De Fide Haereticis servanda, Martini Becani.* Amsterdam, 1608.

Germanus, Francus [pseud.]. *Repraesentatio pacis generalis.* s.l., 1607.

Junius, Franciscus. *Brief discours envoyé au roy Philippe.* Antwerp, 1566.

Loefenius, Michael. *Wolmeinende Warnung An alle Christliche Potentaten und Obrigkeiten/ Wider Deß Bapsts unnd seiner Jesuiten hochgefehrliche Lehr und Practicken.* Heidelberg, 1606.

Migne, J.-P., ed. *Patrologiae cursus completus: Series latina*. 221 vols. Paris: Migne, 1844–65.

Molanus, Johannes. *Libri quinque, De fide haereticis servanda tres, De fide rebellibus servanda, liber unus, qui est quartus: Item unicus, De fide et iuramento, quae a tyranno exiguntur, qui est quintus*. Cologne, 1584.

Pareus, David. *Acta Colloquiorum Swalbacensium*. Heidelberg, 1618.

———. *In divinam ad Romanos epistolam commentarius*. Heidelberg, 1608.

———. *Oratio inauguralis de fide haereticis servanda*. Heidelberg, 1618.

Plancius, Daniel. *Dissertatio de fide haereticis non servanda*. Amsterdam, 1608.

———. *Reden-strijd van de Ketters ghenn gheloove te houden*. Amsterdam, 1609.

Rosweyde, Heribert. *De fide haereticis servanda*. Antwerp, 1610.

Sweerts, Robert. *De fide haereticis servanda*. Antwerp, 1611.

Thyraeus, Petrus. *De libertate fidei religionis Christianae disputatio theologica tripartita*. Mainz, 1590.

Ungersdorff, Christoph von [Caspar Schoppe]. *Erinnerung von der Calvinisten falschen betrüglichen Art und Feindseligkeit gegen dem heiligen Römischen Reich. Item/ Widerholung der Catholischen Scribenten/ sonderlich der Herrn Jesuiter Lehr und Meynung vom Religions Frieden/ und ob Ketzern/ Trew und Glaub zu halten sey*. s.l., 1616.

Secondary Sources

Arndt, Johannes. *Das Heilige Römische Reich und die Niederlande 1566 bis 1648: Politisch-konfessionelle Verflechtung und Publizistik im Achtzigjährigen Krieg*. Cologne: Böhlau, 1998.

Becker, Michael. *Kriegsrecht im frühneuzeitlichen Protestantismus: Eine Untersuchung zum Beitrag lutherischer und reformierter Theologen, Juristen und anderer Gelehrter zur Kriegsrechtsliteratur im 16. und 17. Jahrhundert*. Tübingen: Mohr Siebeck, 2017.

Braun, Harald. *Juan de Mariana and Early Modern Spanish Political Thought*. Aldershot, UK: Ashgate, 2011.

Decock, Wim. *Theologians and Contract Law: The Moral Transformation of the Ius Commune (ca. 1500–1650)*. Leiden: Brill, 2013.

———. "Trust Beyond Faith: Re-Thinking Contracts with Heretics and Excommunicates in Times of Religious War." *Rivista Internazionale di Diritto Comune* 27 (2016): 301–28.

Dienst, Tobias. "Das 'Schwalbacher Kolloquium' 1608 und sein publizistisches Nachspiel: Mündliche und schriftliche interkonfessionelle Kommunikation vor dem Dreißigjährigen Krieg." *Jahrbuch der Hessischen Kirchengeschichtlichen Vereinigung* 68 (2017): 201–35.

Döllinger, Ignaz von, and Franz Heinrich Reusch, eds. *Geschichte der Moralstreitigkeiten in der römisch-catholischen Kirche*. 2 vols. Nördlingen: Beck, 1889.

Dreitzel, Horst. "Toleranz und Gewissensfreiheit im konfessionellen Zeitalter: Zur Diskussion im Reich zwischen Augsburger Religionsfrieden und Aufklärung." In *Religion und Religiosität im Zeitalter des Barock*, edited by Dieter Breuer, vol. 1, 115–28. Wiesbaden: Harrassowitz, 1995.

Duhr, Bernhard. *Geschichte der Jesuiten in den Ländern deutscher Zunge*. Vol. 2. Part 2. Freiburg: Herder, 1913.

———. *Jesuiten-Fabeln: Ein Beitrag zur Kulturgeschichte*. 4th ed. Freiburg: Herder, 1904.

Fabre, Pierre-Antoine, and Catherine Maire, eds. *Les antijésuites: Discours, figures et lieux de l'antijésuitisme à l'époque modern*. Rennes: Presses Universitaires, 2010.

Forst, Rainer. *Toleration in Conflict: Past and Present*. Translated by Ciaran Cronin. Cambridge: Cambridge University Press, 2013.

Friedeburg, Robert von, and Michael Seidler. "The Holy Roman Empire of the German Nation." In *European Political Thought 1450–1700: Religion, Law and Philosophy*, edited by Howell A. Lloyd, Glenn Burgess, and Simon Hodson, 102–75. New Haven, CT: Yale University Press, 2007.

Fudge, Thomas A. *The Trial of Jan Hus: Medieval Heresy and Criminal Procedure*. Oxford: Oxford University Press, 2013.

Gabel, Helmut. "Glaube—Individuum—Reichsrecht: Toleranzdenken im Reich von Augsburg bis Münster." In *Krieg und Kultur: Die Rezeption von Krieg und Frieden in der Niederländischen Republik und im Deutschen Reich*, edited by Horst Lademacher and Simon Groenveld, 157–77. Münster: Waxmann, 1998.

Guggisberg, Hans R. "Wandel der Argumente für religiöse Toleranz und Glaubensfreiheit im 16. und 17. Jahrhundert." In *Zur Geschichte der Toleranz und Religionsfreiheit*, edited by Heinrich Lutz, 455–81. Darmstadt: WBG, 1977.

Happel, Otto. *Katholisches und Protestantisches Christentum nach der Auffassung der alten katholischen Polemik insbesondere des Martinus Becanus.* Würzburg: Göbel, 1898.

Höpfl, Harro. *Jesuit Political Thought: The Society of Jesus and the State, c. 1540–1630.* Cambridge: Cambridge University Press, 2004.

Hotson, Howard. "Irenicism in the Confessional Age: The Holy Roman Empire, 1563–1648." In *Conciliation and Confession: The Struggle for Unity in the Age of Reform, 1415–1648*, edited by Howard Louthan and Randall C. Zachman, 228–85. Notre Dame, IN: Notre Dame University Press, 2004.

Kaplan, Benjamin. *Divided by Faith: Religious Conflict and the Practice of Toleration in Early Modern Europe.* Cambridge, MA: Belknap Press, 2007.

Kooi, Christine. *Calvinists and Catholics during Holland's Golden Age: Heretics and Idolaters.* Cambridge: Cambridge University Press, 2012.

———. "Paying Off the Sheriff: Strategies of Catholic Toleration in Golden Age Holland." In *Calvinism and Religious Toleration in the Dutch Golden Age*, edited by R. Po-Chia Hsia and Henk Van Nierop, 87–101. Cambridge: Cambridge University Press, 2002.

Krebs, Richard. *Die politische Publizistik der Jesuiten und ihrer Gegner: In den letzten Jahrzehnten vor Ausbruch des Dreißigjährigen Krieges.* Halle: Niemeyer, 1890.

Lecler, Joseph. *Histoire de la tolérance au siècle de la réforme.* Paris: Montaigne, 1955.

Lesaffer, Randall, ed. *The Twelve Years Truce (1609): Peace, Truce, War and Law in the Low Countries at the Turn of the 17th Century.* Leiden: Brill, 2014.

Paintner, Ursula. *'Des Papsts neue Creatur': Antijesuitische Publizistik im Deutschsprachigen Raum, 1555-1618.* Amsterdam: Rodopi, 2011.

Pettegree, Andrew. "The Politics of Toleration in the Free Netherlands, 1572-1620." In *Tolerance and Intolerance in the European Reformation*, edited by Ole Peter Grell and Bob Scribner, 182-98. Cambridge: Cambridge University Press, 1996.

Salatowsky, Sascha. "Zwischen Hinrichtung und Duldung: Toleranzdebatten im konfessionellen Zeitalter, 1580-1650." *Deutsche Zeitschrift für Philosophie* 63, no. 1 (2015): 22-57.

Schneider, Bernd Christian. Ius Reformandi: *Die Entwicklung des Staatskirchenrechts von seinen Anfängen bis zum Ende des Alten Reiches.* Tübingen: Mohr Siebeck, 2001.

Schreiner, Klaus. "Toleranz." In vol. 6 of *Geschichtliche Grundbegriffe*, edited by O. Brunner, W. Conze, and R. Koselleck, 445-605. Stuttgart: Klett, 1990.

Sibeth, Uwe. "Der 'Friede' als Fortsetzung des Krieges mit anderen Mitteln: Zur Representatio pacis generalis (1607) des Pieter Cornelisz Brederode." In *Wege der Neuzeit: Festschrift für Heinz Schilling zum 65. Geburtstag*, ed. Stefan Ehrenpreis, Ute Lotz-Heumann, Olaf Mörke, and Luise Schorn-Schütte, 479-502. Berlin: Duncker und Humblot, 2007.

Stieve, Felix. *Die Politik Baierns 1591-1607: Zweite Hälfte.* Munich: Rieger, 1883.

Strohm, Christoph. *Calvinismus und Recht: Weltanschaulich-konfessionelle Aspekte im Werk reformierter Juristen in der Frühen Neuzeit.* Tübingen: Mohr Siebeck, 2008.

———. "Konfessionsspezifische Zugänge zum Augsburger Religionsfrieden bei lutherischen, reformierten und katholischen Juristen." In *Der Augsburger Religionsfrieden 1555*, edited by Heinz Schilling and Heribert Smolinsky, 127-56. Gütersloh: Gütersloher Verlagshaus, 2007.

Strohmeyer, Arno. *Konfessionskonflikt und Herrschaftsordnung. Widerstandsrecht bei den österreichischen Ständen (1550-1650).* Mainz: Philipp von Zabern, 2006.

Tutino, Stefania. *Empire of Souls: Robert Bellarmine and the Christian Commonwealth.* Oxford: Oxford University Press, 2010.

Zagorin, Perez. *How the Idea of Religious Toleration Came to the West.* Princeton, NJ: Princeton University Press, 2003.

Zwierlein, Cornel. Discorso und Lex Dei: *Die Entstehung neuer Denkrahmen im 16. Jahrhundert und die Wahrnehmung der französischen Religionskriege in Italien und Deutschland.* Göttingen: Vandenhoeck & Ruprecht, 2006.

Translator's Note

The source text used for this translation is the Mainz 1614 edition of *De fide haereticis servanda*, which is included in the second volume of Becanus's minor theological works (*Opuscula theologica*). It is available online through the State Library of Bavaria in Munich.[1] Except for typographical mistakes, we have not observed any substantial differences between this edition and the first edition of 1607. In translating the Latin, we have attempted to keep as closely as possible to the original text, sometimes preferring a more literal translation over an elegant modern English style. Citations from the Bible follow the Vulgate numbering used by Becanus. Scripture translations are ours, although we have drawn inspiration from the Douay-Rheims and King James English translations.[2] Translations of quotations from classical and patristic sources, which Becanus often cites in a fragmentary way, are also ours. References to the letters of Ambrose, Augustine, and Pope Leo the Great follow modern numbering. Similarly, Becanus's citations of legal and theological sources, which are located in the body text of his work, have been set as footnotes in this edition and have been rendered according to modern citation conventions. Special attention has been paid to rendering technical legal vocabulary consistently. Several Latin words associated with the English term "agreement" have been translated each in their own way so that the reader may

---

[1] http://mdz-nbn-resolving.de/urn:nbn:de:bvb:12-bsb10772321-8.

[2] www.latinvulgate.com.

Translator's Note

recognize the technical nature of the Latin words used by Becanus: "promise" corresponds to *promissio*, "offer" to *pollicitatio*, "agreement" to *pactum*, "contract" to *contractus*, "deal" to *conventum*, "bargain" to *conventio*, and "treaty" to *foedus*. The English "licit" corresponds to the Latin *licitum*, while "experts" is the translation of *doctores*. The word *malum* has been rendered as "evil" when combined with *intrinsice* or *ex natura*. For all other matters of citation or translation, the reader is kindly requested to consult the editorial notes (introduced by "Ed. note:").

I would like to thank my dear friend Sarah Kim for proofreading the English text and for the enthusiasm she expressed for this work, and my dear friends Sandra Post and Alexandr Komkov for their moral support. Lastly, I would like to thank Tuut, who was lying on my arm a lot of the time while I was translating and caused me to type with one hand. She was a wonderful support.

— Isabelle Buhre

Abbreviations

Cod.	Corpus Iuris Civilis, Codex
Dig.	Corpus Iuris Civilis, Digesta
Inst.	Corpus Iuris Civilis, Institutiones
Dec. Grat.	Corpus Iuris Canonici, Decretum Gratiani
Dec. Greg.	Corpus Iuris Canonici, Decretales Gregorii IX
Liber Sextus	Corpus Iuris Canonici, Decretales Bonifatii VIII
PL	*Patrologiae cursus completus: Series latina.* Edited by J.-P. Migne. 221 vols. Paris: Migne, 1844–65.

On the Duty to Keep Faith with Heretics

To the Reader

In discussions about keeping faith, two mistakes are common. The first we find among the *politiques* of our time,[1] who generally believe they can betray faith and oath whenever it seems useful to them. Both Pedro de Ribadeneira[2] and Justus Lipsius[3] argue against

---

[1] Ed. note: The word *politiques* refers to an eclectic group of jurists and intellectuals in late sixteenth-century France who put the interests of the state over and above concerns about uniformity of religious doctrine. The movement gained momentum after the outbreak of the first religious war between Protestants and Catholics in France in 1562 and influenced King Henry IV's Edict of Nantes (1598). More generally, the term came to denote pragmatic thinkers and political actors willing to forsake religious principles for the sake of political expediency and "reason of state." The Jesuits commonly equated *politiques* with Machiavellians. Harro Höpfl, *Jesuit Political Thought: The Society of Jesus and the State, c. 1540–1630* (Cambridge: Cambridge University Press, 2004), 99.

[2] Pedro de Ribadeneira, *The Christian Prince* 2.15. Ed. note: Ribadeneira (1527–1611), a Jesuit, authored "Treatise on the Religion and the Virtues That a Christian Prince Should Have," an important mirror for princes offering advice to pious leaders on how they could make political decisions consonant with Christian virtues. He was one of the sharpest critics of the *politiques*, considering them even worse than Machiavelli in subordinating religion to politics. Nicole Reinhardt, *Voices of Conscience: Royal Confessors and Political Counsel in Seventeenth-Century Spain and France* (Oxford: Oxford University Press, 2016), 39–40.

[3] Ed. note: Lipsius (1547–1606), jurist, philologist, poet, and historian, is considered one of the greatest humanists of the Low Countries. Jan Papy, "Justus Lipsius," *The Stanford Encyclopedia of Philosophy* (Fall 2011 edition), https://plato.stanford.edu/archives/fall2011/entries/justus-lipsius/. Drawing

those thinkers. Among other things, Lipsius writes the following:[4]

> And where do we find these new learned men? "Wherever there is no altar, no faith, and no stable contract."[5]
>
> They poison the ears of our princes and encourage them "to neglect anything right and honorable, as long as they can stay in power."[6]
>
> And meanwhile they keep repeating the same old phrase,
>> "for the sake of governance
>> the law must be violated. Save your piety for other areas of life."[7]
>
> Woe to them! They are idle and mistaken. For "no necessity can force us to betray our faith, nor is it bought for any price."[8]
>> "It is more powerful
>> than kingdoms glittering in purple glow."[9]

---

on a synthesis of Stoic virtue ethics and biblical principles, he offered a Christian alternative to Machiavellian reason of state in his writings "On Constance" (1584), "On Politics" (1589), and "Political Admonitions and Examples" (1605). See Erik De Bom, Marijke Janssens, Toon Van Houdt, and Jan Papy, eds., *(Un)Masking the Realities of Power: Justus Lipsius and the Dynamics of Political Writing in Early Modern Europe* (Leiden: Brill, 2011).

[4] Justus Lipsius, *Politica* 2.14. Ed. note: Lipsius's *Politica* takes the form of a *cento*, that is, a "patchwork" of citations from mostly classical authors. Becanus quotes from the *Politica* without including Lipsius's references to his sources. We have therefore provided references to the sources on which Lipsius's quotations are based following the edition by Jan Waszink. See Justus Lipsius, *Politica: Six Books of Politics or Political Instruction*, ed. Jan Waszink (Assen: Van Gorcum, 2004), 333–35.

[5] Ed. note: Aristophanes, *The Acharnians* 308.

[6] Ed. note: Cicero, *On Duties* 3.82.

[7] Ed. note: Euripides, *The Phoenician Women* 524–25.

[8] Ed. note: Seneca, *Epistles* 88.29.

[9] Ed. note: Silius Italicus, *Punica* 13.285–86.

They mix up fraud and fallacies. I know that. And "the faithless will never run out of reasons why they do not keep their promise."[10] "They always put an appearance of justice on fraud."[11]

But may they listen to the great Brasidas: "It is even more scandalous if those in high positions surround and damage what is honorable with fraud than with plain violence."[12]

Some assume "there is no faith when it has been given to a faithless person."[13]

They are mistaken "and seek a feigned excuse for their perjury."[14]

For "even to faithless people we must keep our faith,"[15]

Even in wartime, and,

> "he is the best
> warrior, who in the first and the last place,
> amid conflict, keeps protecting faith."[16]

Therefore, away with them, my kings!

> "and do not break the treatises of peace
> and do not put your kingdom before faith."[17]

---

[10] Ed. note: Livy, *History of Rome* 9.11.6.

[11] Ed. note: Livy, *History of Rome* 9.11.7.

[12] Ed. note: Thucydides, *History of the Peloponnesian War* 4.86.6.

[13] Ed. note: Cicero, *On Duties* 3.106.

[14] Ed. note: Cicero, *On Duties* 3.106.

[15] Ed. note: Ambrose, *On Duties*, 3.10. The reference in Lipsius's text is actually to the second book of *On Duties*, leading Waszink to suggest 2.7.33, but he rightly doubts that this is correct.

[16] Ed. note: Silius Italicus, *Punica* 14.169–71.

[17] Ed. note: Silius Italicus, *Punica* 2.700–701.

Reflect on this, "not to perjure yourself, fearful of both divine vengeance and human dishonor."[18]

Assuredly,

"And even if one manages to hide his perfidy at first, late punishment will come on silent feet."[19]

Thus Lipsius writes in his *Politica*.

The second error is made by those who believe one should keep his faith with everyone except heretics. Johannes Molanus,[20] a doctor of theology and professor in Louvain, went extensively against them in three little books, which he called *On the Duty to Keep Faith with Heretics*. However, these books have been out of print for a couple of years now, and only a few people still possess and read them. Therefore, I thought it would be worthwhile to write a disputation on the same topic, in the scholastic manner and based on stable and legitimate grounds, and set out the entire controversy clearly and transparently.

Farewell, my reader. May you regard me favorably.

---

[18] Ed. note: Pseudo-Aristotle [Anaximenes of Lampsacus], *Rhetoric to Alexander* 17.1 (1432a35–37).

[19] Ed. note: Tibullus, *Carmina* 1.9.4.

[20] Ed. note: Johannes Molanus (1533–1585) taught theology at the Catholic University of Louvain. He is mostly remembered for his work on the dogmatics of Christian iconography, but he also wrote a treatise on the duty to keep faith with heretics, published in Cologne in 1585. Although Molanus's and Becanus's titles are the same, Molanus's earlier treatise is less juridical and more biblical in nature than that of Becanus.

Theological Disputation: Should One Keep His Faith with Heretics?

1. The word *faith*, as St. Thomas already noted in his commentary on the *Sentences*, is used in several ways.[1] First, it is used to denote the Catholic faith, through which we believe to be true what God has revealed: "Without faith it is impossible to please God" (Heb. 11:6). Second, we use it to describe human faith or credulity. Terence writes in his *Andria*, "I almost took faith in you."[2] Third, *faith* can be used to describe good or bad conscience. Legal experts use it in this way when they say "a defendant of good faith, not of bad." The fourth meaning concerns faithfulness in keeping promises and honoring deals: "Persist in keeping your faith with us" (1 Macc. 10:27). In my disputation, I will talk only about this last usage of *faith*.

2. Taking a look at the etymology of the word *faith*, or *fides* in Latin, it is said to come from *fio* (to happen) and *dico* (to say), as if that which has been said happens because of faith. Cicero attests this.[3] In his nineteenth letter to Jerome, Augustine writes along the same lines: "The word 'faith' in the Latin language is said to be called *fides* because what is being said happens."[4] If you take a close look, you will see Cicero defines it at the place I mentioned in the following way: "Faith is the correspondence with and truthfulness to words and deals."

---

[1] Thomas Aquinas, *On the Sentences* 3.12.

[2] Terence, *Andria* 3.4.7.

[3] Cicero, *On Duties* 1.23.

[4] Augustine, *Letters*, 82.2.22.

After all, words and deals correspond with reality and turn out to be true if that which has been said or bargained happens.

3. Therefore, the question is this: Should one keep his faith with heretics in promises, agreements, and deals? Catholics answer this question with a resolute yes, regardless of whether it concerns promises, agreements, or contracts, as long as they are licit and honorable. In short: the fact that some people are heretics and others Catholics does not diminish the obligation of keeping your faith with either of them and to stick to what has been promised or captured in contract. For example: in the imperial council, you concluded an agreement on the same matter with two kings, one of them a Catholic, the other a heretic. If the agreement has been lawfully concluded otherwise, you will have to keep your faith no less to the latter than to the former. This is our point of view.

4. Our opponents make two mistakes here. First, they attribute the exact opposite opinion to us. They say we preach one should *not* keep his faith with heretics, which is a plain lie. In this respect they resemble the Pharisees who, even though they had heard the words coming from Christ's own mouth, "Therefore render to Caesar the things that are Caesar's, and to God the things that are God's" (Matt. 22:21), still dared to slander him in front of Pilate: "We found this man plotting against our people and prohibiting to pay tributes to Caesar" (Luke 23:2). Clearly, this is the way our opponents treat us. Both publicly and privately, in spoken and in written word, we teach and we testify *one should keep his faith with heretics*, and still they keep shouting wherever they go, "We found these people denying one should keep his faith with heretics!"

5. And they do not leave it at that. They use this lie as a cover, as if now they were allowed to repeal and violate agreements they themselves made with Catholics. Again, they are similar to the Pharisees. They shouted, "Crucify him, crucify him!" What wrong did he do? "We heard him prohibiting to pay tributes to Caesar." In the same way, our opponents yell, "Repeal the faith you gave to Catholics; repeal agreements reached with Catholics." Why? "We heard them preaching one should not keep his faith with heretics. So why should we keep

our faith with them?" It is obvious: just as the Pharisees covered their murder with a lie, our opponents lie to cover up their perfidy.

6. But to the point: I must explain three different things here. First, I will go through some general teachings on which the settlement of this entire controversy depends. Second, I will use each of them to show in detail why we should keep our faith with heretics no less than with Catholics. Third, I will investigate a few particular cases that present us with some more difficulties. I will point out all these things in the following order:

The Chapters of This Disputation

1. Three types of promise: gratuitous, onerous, and under oath
2. Under which circumstances is a gratuitous promise valid?
3. Under which circumstances is an onerous promise valid?
4. Under which circumstances is a promise under oath valid?
5. Where does the obligation of a valid promise come from?
6. How great is the obligation of a valid promise?
7. In the case of a valid promise with obligatory force, do we have to keep our faith with heretics, given the fact that they are heretics?
8. Do we have to keep our faith with them when they have been excommunicated?
9. Do we also have to keep our faith with them in marriage contracts?
10. And when it comes to freedom of religion?
11. And in wartime?
12. And regarding safe conduct?

These and similar problems are encountered in daily practice, and many people are perplexed by them. Therefore, I will explain shortly what needs to be said about each of them separately.

1

Three Types of Promise: Gratuitous, Onerous, and Under Oath

1. There are two types of promise: one type is made to God, the other to man. The former is called *vow*; St. Thomas has already spoken about this.[1] The latter bears the actual name *promise*. This second type of promise—the only one we shall discuss—receives various names among legal experts. After all, it is not only called *offer*[2] but also *agreement*,[3] as well as *stipulation*.[4] We use the term *offer* when something is merely offered by a person who makes a promise. The word *agreement* is used when the promisee accepts the offer. Ulpian explains this difference: "An agreement is the mutual consent of two parties. An offer, by contrast, is the promise of the person who makes an offer solely."[5] Theologians also discuss this topic: "An offer is a plain promise not yet followed by an acceptance; an agreement, however, is

---

[1] Thomas Aquinas, *Summa theologiae* II.2, Q. 88.
[2] *pollicitatio*.
[3] *pactum*.
[4] *stipulatio*.
[5] Dig. 50.12.3*pr*.

an accepted promise."[6] When a promise and an acceptance are made through a certain formula (first the question of one person, followed by the reply of the other), legal experts call it a *stipulation*. To give you some examples:

> Do you promise to give me that much?
> Yes, I do.
>
> Do you promise one thousand?
> Yes, I do.
>
> Will you give me one thousand for my house?
> Yes, I will.

And so on.

2. A promise made to man can take three forms. First, there is the gratuitous, or free, promise, which puts an obligation only on the person who makes it. This is the case with donations. Second, there is the onerous promise, carrying obligatory force for both parties. This is the case with contracts in the strict sense of the word,[7] both public and private ones.[8] The third type is the promise under oath. No matter whether it originally started off as gratuitous or onerous, this type of promise is stronger because it has been confirmed with an oath. In the following chapters I will proceed along the lines of this distinction and deal with each of these types successively.

---

[6] Ed. note: For references to specific theologians defending the proposition that agreements are accepted promises, see Wim Decock, *Theologians and Contract Law: The Moral Transformation of the* Ius Commune *(ca. 1500–1650)* (Leiden: Brill, 2013), 187–92.

[7] *contractibus*.

[8] Ed. note: Contracts, in the strict sense of binding agreements (*contractus*), were limited to onerous or synallagmatic agreements, according to an influential definition by Marcus Antistius Labeo (c. first century BC/first century AD), a Roman jurist. His definition of *contractus* was included in Justinian's Digest; cf. Dig. 50.16.19. The scholastic view that all accepted promises are binding, regardless of whether they lead to a synallagmatic agreement or not, made the distinction between contracts in the proper sense of the word and other types of agreements largely superfluous.

2

Under Which Circumstances Is a Gratuitous Promise Valid?

1. For a gratuitous or free promise to be valid and to carry any obligatory force, there are some requirements to be met by the person who makes the promise, some others by the person to whom the promise is made, and some by the thing that is being promised.

2. The requirements for the person who makes the promise are the following: (1) that he is able to commit himself, (2) that he wants and has the intention to commit himself, (3) that he does so thoughtfully and deliberately, and (4) that he does so freely and voluntarily. For when a promise has been made under violent pressure or out of fear, we are not obliged to fulfill it if no oath has been taken, as St. Thomas has taught.[1] The reason for this is that if someone wrenches out a promise by fear or by force, he is doing injustice. On the grounds of injustice, the person who made the promise does not have to fulfill it.[2]

---

[1] Thomas Aquinas, *Summa theologiae* II.2, Q. 89, A. 7, ad 4.

[2] See below chapter 3, no. 6.

3. The requirement for the person to whom the promise is made is that he accepts it. Before a naked promise[3] becomes an agreement—which happens through acceptance—it normally does not bear any obligatory force and cannot lead to a right to sue in the civil court. This opinion is widely accepted, as Gómez testifies.[4] The reason for this is that there can be no obligation unless through mutual consent of both parties.[5] Consequently, it is possible to revoke a promise before its acceptance, which we can directly deduce from Roman law.[6]

4. I said "normally," because there are a few exceptions of simple offers[7] bearing force before their acceptance, especially those made to a municipality regarding the restoration of buildings or on the occasion of honorary offices received or to be received by it or regarding works that have already been started (see the passage on unilateral offers in the Digest in its entirety).[8] Some authors

---

[3] Ed. note: A "naked" promise (*nuda promissio*) is a technical term used by scholastic theologians to designate a simple promise that has no binding effect. Similarly a "naked" or "bare" agreement (*nudum pactum, nuda pactio*) is a technical legal term going back to Roman law (Dig. 2.14.7.4) meaning that the agreement cannot be enforced in court. By contrast, if a deal has been "clothed" (*pactum vestititum*), for instance because it has been confirmed by an oath, then it is considered binding; see Wim Decock, *Theologians and Contract Law: The Moral Transformation of the* Ius Commune *(ca. 1500–1650)* (Leiden: Brill, 2013), 110–12.

[4] Antonio Gómez (Gomezius), *Commentaries and Various Resolutions from the Common and Royal Civil Law* 2.9.1. Ed. note: The requirement of acceptance is discussed in Decock, *Theologians and Contract Law*, 187. Gómez (c. 1501–1561), a jurist heavily influenced by Thomistic thought, held the chair of Roman law at the University of Salamanca. His interpretation of Justinian's legal texts was held in high esteem by scholastic theologians in the Spanish empire and beyond throughout the early modern period.

[5] Dig. 2.14.1.

[6] Dig. 39.5.10; Dig. 40.2.4pr.

[7] *pollicitationes.*

[8] Dig. 50.12.

even add promises made to a collective entity with a legal personality,[9] a church or a hospital, because promises made for pious causes seem equal to those made to a municipality, if we take into account their privileges according to Roman imperial law.[10]

5. The requirement for the subject of the promise is that it is licit and honorable. If this is not the case, the promise is invalid. We know this on the basis of the law "Agreements" in the chapter on agreements in Justinian's Code, which reads as follows: "There is no doubt in law that agreements going against laws, imperial constitutions, or good morals carry no force whatsoever."[11] From this provision we can deduce two rules that are very useful in this matter.

6. This is the first rule: all promises and agreements whose fulfillment is illicit and prohibited by law are invalid according to divine and natural law—for example, if you promised you would steal something, commit murder or adultery, turn to the heresy of Luther or Calvin, or neglect the confession of sins and all other sacraments. The reason for this is no one can be obliged to sin. Isidore writes about this and is cited by Gratian: "Repeal your faith in case of wrong promises."[12] And further on in the same canon: "A promise fulfilled in a criminal way is impious." It does not make any difference whether an additional oath has been taken or not. It will be made in vain, for "an oath cannot be a bond of injustice"; that is to say, it cannot oblige one to evil, as is evident from Molina.[13]

---

[9] *universitas*.

[10] Cod. 1.2.19 and Cod. 1.2.23*pr*.

[11] Cod. 2.3.6.

[12] Dec. Grat. C.22 q.4 c.5. Ed. note: Along with Liber Sextus *reg. iur.* 39, this passage was a standard argument adduced to demonstrate the invalidity of immoral promises. See Decock, *Theologians and Contract Law*, 424 and 481–82.

[13] Luis de Molina, *On Justice and Right*, 2.271. Ed. note: Luis de Molina SJ (1535–1600) taught theology at the University of Evora but was heavily influenced by the renaissance of Thomism at Salamanca. He was the first Jesuit to write a treatise *On Justice and Right*, the second volume of which was dedicated to contract law in the context of the virtue of commutative

7. This is the second rule: all promises and agreements whose fulfillment goes against good morals are invalid according to civil law. Among these are all promises providing an opportunity to sin—for example, when you promise the other party that he will not be held liable for deceit, duress, injustice, or theft.[14] The same applies to the promises taking away one's liberty to dispose of one's possessions at will—for example, if you promise someone to make him your heir and refrain from altering your testament in the future. See again Molina at the place I mentioned. But does one still have to hold to these kinds of promises and agreements, which go against good morals and are therefore invalid under civil law, before the tribunal of conscience, if they have been made under oath? I will discuss this question in chapter 4.

---

justice. See Diego Alonso-Lasheras, *Luis de Molina's* De iustitia et iure: *Justice as Virtue in an Economic Context* (Leiden: Brill, 2011).

[14] Dig. 2.14.27.

3

UNDER WHICH CIRCUMSTANCES IS AN ONEROUS PROMISE VALID?

1. For an onerous promise, like the ones we find in contracts,[1] to be valid and to carry any obligatory force, a few requirements are to be met. (1) The people who make the promise on both sides must be able to oblige themselves. (2) They must want and have the intention to oblige themselves. (3) They must do so thoughtfully and deliberately. (4) They must do so freely and voluntarily—that is, without force or fear, without deception or fraud. (5) The subject of the agreement must be licit and honorable. These requirements are crystal clear. Only about the fourth condition two questions might arise: one about the force and fear, the other about mistake and deceit.

2. *The first question.* Does a promise or a contract have to be so spontaneous and voluntary that it excludes any force or fear in order to be valid? I am talking about great fear, which may even seize a firm man. This type of fear may strike one justly or unjustly. It strikes one justly when we are able to inflict the bad we are threatening by law,

---

[1] *contractibus*. Ed. note: On the term *contractus*, see p. 12n8.

and unjustly if we are not able to do so. Having said this, let me move on to the first conclusion.

3. *The first conclusion.* If you have been forced to sign a contract or make a promise under great fear but still justly, the contract is valid. This view is widely accepted. In this way a person who got engaged for fear of excommunication can still be compelled to marry, and this marriage contract will be valid.[2] Someone who raped a girl will be obliged to either endow or marry her. And if someone made a promise to another person in order to escape being accused of a crime that could rightly be brought against him, he is obliged to honor it.

The reason behind this is that fear of this kind does not make a contract involuntary in an absolute sense, for a person who entered into a contract like this agreed with it completely. He has taken everything into consideration, and then he *wants* it. Therefore, since no injustice intervenes, the contract will be valid.

4. *The second conclusion.* If someone has been unjustly forced to conclude a contract or to make a promise under great fear, the contract is still not entirely invalid according to both natural and positive law. However, it can be revoked and declared invalid in accordance with the judgment of the person who unjustly suffered from the fear inflicted on him. This conclusion consists of three different parts. *The first part* is: a contract of this sort is not entirely invalid under natural law. This is what Domingo de Soto,[3] Pierre de la Palud,[4] and other authors assert.

---

[2] Dec. Greg. 4.1.10.

[3] Domingo de Soto, *On the Sentences* 4.29.1.3. Ed. note: Soto (1495–1560) was a Dominican friar and theologian at the University of Salamanca. He wrote an influential commentary on Peter Lombard's *Sentences*, but he is even better known as the author of the first treatise *On Justice and Right*. Along with Francisco de Vitoria, he is remembered as one of the protagonists of the School of Salamanca. See Benjamin Hill, "Domingo de Soto," in *Great Christian Jurists in Spanish History*, ed. Rafael Domingo and Javier Martínez-Torrón (Cambridge: Cambridge University Press, 2018), 134–56.

[4] Pierre de la Palud, *On the Sentences* 4.15.2.5. Ed. note: Pierre de la Palud (Paludanus, c. 1275–1342) entered the Dominican order and became a profes-

The reason is that the invalidity of a contract under natural law must either originate from a lack of consent or from a certain intervening injustice. A lack of consent cannot be the ground because when someone is being forced to make a promise under just fear, the agreement will be valid on the basis of consent, as has been said before. The same reasoning applies in the case of unjustly inflicted fear. Injustice cannot be a ground either because this is not the immediate cause of the contract, the immediate cause being the consent of the contracting party. Therefore, when there is sufficient consent, the contract will be valid, although it can be revoked on the grounds of injustice, as I shall explain below.

5. *The second part* is: a contract of this sort is not entirely invalid under positive law. This is what Dr. Navarrus, along with other authors, writes.[5] We can find proof of this in civil law in Justinian's Institutes: "If, in a stipulation, you made a promise you should not have made to Titius and you were coerced by fear, deceived, or mistaken in doing so, it is clear you are still obliged to your promise under civil law; and the action on your promise to give is efficacious."[6] The gloss on this passages says, "You are obliged, certainly, according to the rigor of the law; and the action is efficacious, as far as its substance is concerned." This same point is made in the Digest: "If I acquired someone's heritage while being coerced by fear, I think that I have become its heir,

---

sor of theology at the University of Paris. His commentary on the *Sentences* was still popular among the early modern scholastics. Jean Dunbabin, *A Hound of God: Pierre de la Palud and the Fourteenth-Century* (Oxford: Oxford University Press, 1991).

[5] Dr. Navarrus, *Relection on canon* Accepta (Dec. Greg. 2.13.3), oppositio 5.7. Ed. note: Martín de Azpilcueta (1492–1586) was also referred to as Dr. Navarrus by his contemporaries because he was born in the kingdom of Navarra. Along with Diego de Covarrubias y Leyva, his student, Dr. Navarrus counts as one of the most important canon lawyers in the early modern Spanish empire and beyond. He taught at the Universities of Salamanca and Coimbra. See Wim Decock, "Martín de Azpilcueta," in *Great Christian Jurists in Spanish History*, ed. Domingo and Martínez-Torrón, 116–33.

[6] Inst. 4.13.

because even though I would not have wanted it if it had been a free choice, I still wanted it while being coerced. However, I should obtain restitution from the praetor; he should grant me the power to abstain from it."[7] We can find similar evidence in the Code of Justinian[8] and in the *Liber Sextus* of Pope Boniface VIII.[9]

Nevertheless, there are some exceptional cases in which fear does make promises and pacts entirely invalid. See the gloss on the *Liber Sextus* and Lessius.[10]

6. *The third part* is: such a contract can be revoked at the option of the person who unjustly suffered from fear. Hence we find these words in the canon law: "Things taking place by force or under fear must be declared invalid; they must lack any firm power."[11] And in Roman law we read, "We order any selling, donation, or transaction that came into being by force to be invalidated."[12] The reason for this is that a person who unjustly inflicted fear on someone else did injustice to another person. As a result, he is obliged to bring him back to the state he was in before, and the other person has a right to claim this restitution. That is the meaning of the passage from the Digest cited earlier: "I should obtain restitution from the praetor; he should grant me the power to abstain from it."[13]

---

[7] Dig. 4.2.21*pr*.

[8] Cod. 2.19.12.

[9] Liber Sextus 1.20.2 and 4.

[10] Lessius, *On Justice and Right* 2.17.6. Ed. note: Leonardus Lessius SJ (1554–1623) taught theology at the Jesuit College in Louvain. He studied with Francisco Suárez in Rome and brought the neoscholastic revival home to the Low Countries. His treatise *On Justice and Right* is a masterpiece of moral, legal, and economic thought. See Wim Decock, introduction to *On Sale, Securities, and Insurance*, by Leonardus Lessius, trans. Wim Decock and Nicholas De Sutter (Grand Rapids, MI: CLP Academic, 2016), xxi–l.

[11] Liber Sextus 1.20.2 and 4.

[12] Cod. 2.19.12.

[13] Dig. 4.2.21*pr*.

7. So much for the first question. This is the *second question*: Does a contract have to be entirely free from any deceit or mistake in order to be valid? Deceit or mistake may concern two different aspects: (1) the substance of the thing or (2) one of its qualities. Moreover, the fraud may provide the cause for the contract in such a way that without it you would not have wanted to enter into the contract. It may also not provide the cause for the contract but be merely incidental, as when you certainly wanted to conclude the contract but not at such a high price. At last, the mistake or deceit may either come from one of the contracting parties or from a third party. In the latter case, the contracting party is not involved in bringing about the mistake or deceit. In light of this, I state the following.

8. The *first statement*. If a contract contains a mistake regarding the substance of the thing concerned, the contract shall be invalid according to natural law. This is the case when, for example, a seller believes a gem to be glass, or when a bridegroom thinks Mary is Magdalene, and so on. The reason is that there is no consent on the substance. Your consent is not about the matter that happened to be in the contract by mistake or through deceit, but about something else.

9. The *second statement*. If there is only a mistake regarding the quality of the thing concerned, and if this mistake was not the cause that gave rise to the contract, the contract shall be valid. Domingo de Soto and other authors affirm this.[14] The reason is that when there is true consent on the substance of the matter, this is enough to ensure the validity of the contract, particularly when the deceit concerning the quality did not provide the cause for the contract. For in that case your mind was not opposed to the contract; even if you had known the true quality of the thing, you still would have wanted to conclude the contract, albeit not at this price.

---

[14] Domingo de Soto, *On Justice and Right* 6.3.2. Ed. note: On the huge significance of Soto's *On Justice and Right* for early modern legal, economic, and moral thought, see Wim Decock, "Domingo de Soto: *De iustitia et iure* 1553–1554," in *The Formation and Transmission of Western Legal Culture: 150 Books That Made the Law in the Age of Printing*, ed. Serge Dauchy et al. (Cham: Springer, 2016), 94–96.

10. *The third statement.* If deceit was the cause that gave rise to the contract, and if the deceit was induced by the person who stipulates or enters into a contract with you, the contract is still not entirely invalid according to natural law. However, it may be invalidated at the option of the person who has been deceived, if otherwise the contract can be dissolved. We can derive the fact that it is not entirely invalid plainly from the words I cited above, taken from Justinian's Institutes: "If, in a stipulation, you made a promise you should not have made to Titius and you were coerced by fear, deceived, or mistaken in doing so, it is clear you are still obliged to your promise under civil law; and the action on your promise to give is efficacious." First, we find proof of this in the marriage contract, which is valid even if some deceit regarding the quality intervened. Since by its nature marriage cannot be dissolved, it remains valid. Second, deceit not concerning the substance of the thing cannot undo the nature of the contract. Third, if the deceived person wishes to keep the contract, the deceiver is not allowed to withdraw from it in order to gain any profit from his fraud, as we can read in the canon law;[15] this is a sign that the contract was not entirely invalid.

11. The fact that the contract can still be invalidated at the option of the deceived party is proven as follows. Someone who deceitfully induces another person into concluding a contract does him injustice. Therefore, he is obliged to restore him to his original condition and compensate for anything that might be corrupted, if the deceived person wishes so. At this point there is often discussion about whether a contract of this sort would be entirely invalid according to positive law. After all, it is evident that it is not invalid according to natural law on the basis of the examples I quoted before. Legal experts make this distinction: all contracts of good faith to which deceit by one of the contracting parties has given ground are invalid. However, those contracts which are called *stricti iuris*—all those that come into being in the form of stipulations, along with some others—are valid and bear force in the external court, even if their enforcement can be opposed

---

[15] Dec. Greg. 4.7.1.

by using the *exceptio doli mali*, the legal remedy against bad deceit. For further explanation, see Covarrubias.[16]

12. Others, however, reject this distinction, as if it were legally not well grounded enough. They claim the same rule applies to contracts of good faith and those of strict law: all of them are valid in some way, and all may be opposed by the *exceptio doli mali*. This is the view of Jean Feu, Johannes Faber, and Pierre de Belleperche,[17] cited by Covarrubias at the place I mentioned.[18] The reason is that when fear is the cause that gave rise to the contract, it is not entirely invalid, but it may be declared so, as explained earlier. Yet fear and fraud are considered similar in law, as we can see in both Roman and canon law.[19] Nevertheless, I do not wish to discuss this any further at this point.

13. The *fourth statement*. If mistake or deceit is the cause that gave rise to the contract, and this does not come from the person who stipulates or enters into a contract with you but from some third party or from your own opinion, the contract is absolutely valid. See the gloss

---

[16] Covarrubias, *Commentary on Rule Possessor* 2.6.6. Ed. note: Diego de Covarrubias y Leyva (1512–1577) studied and taught canon law at the University of Salamanca. He wrote influential scholarly works on various aspects of canon law but was also engaged in church governance and legal practice, for instance, as bishop of Segovia and president of the Royal Council of Castile. Richard H. Helmholz, "Diego de Covarrubias y Leyva," in *Great Christian Jurists in Spanish History*, ed. Domingo and Martínez-Torrón, 174–89.

[17] Jean Feu, *Commentary on Dig. 50.17.150*. Ed. note: Pierre de Belleperche (Petrus Bellapertica, c. 1247–1308), Jean Faure (Johannes Faber, c. 1275–1340), and Jean Feu (Johannes Ignaeus, d. 1549) were major French jurists and commentators on Roman law.

[18] Ed. note: Doubts have been raised regarding the authenticity of Covarrubias's arguments from authority in this debate. See Wim Decock, *Theologians and Contract Law: The Moral Transformation of the Ius Commune (ca. 1500–1650)* (Leiden: Brill, 2013), 288.

[19] Cod. 8.38.5; Dec. Greg. 2.24.28.

on canon *Cum dilecti*,[20] Bartolus,[21] Covarrubias,[22] and others. The reason for this is that there is no doubt regarding the substance of the thing contracted for, nor did any injustice from one of the contracting parties intervene, nor is there any right that would render such a contract invalid. Therefore, a person who obtained something by entering into such a contract cannot be obliged to any restitution unless the contract is declared invalid because he has done no injustice at all.

14. However, sincere doubts may arise over the question whether a contract of this sort, after the mistake has been acknowledged, can be rescinded and declared invalid at the option of the deceived person, especially when it is a gratuitous contract, such as a promise or a free gift. Personally, I think it can be revoked because we do not consider a person who spontaneously promises or donates something to do so other than according to the intention that he has while donating or making a promise. Thus, when he has donated or promised something by mistake, he may revoke his promise after having acknowledged the mistake because it was not in line with his intention to donate or promise. But if it is an onerous contract, some authors suppose it cannot be revoked at the option of the deceived person, first, because such a contract does not only depend on the intention and the consent of one person but also on the consent of the other person, who cannot be blamed for the deceit or the mistake; second, because either you have been deceived by your own opinion, and therefore you have to blame yourself for not examining the case any better, or by the fraud

---

[20] Dec. Greg. 3.17.3.

[21] Bartolus, *Commentary on Dig. 4.3.7pr*. Ed. note: Bartolus of Sassoferrato (c. 1313–c. 1358) is one of the most cited medieval commentators on Roman law in the Western legal tradition. An alumnus of the Universities of Bologna and Perugia, he combined a career as a judge with teaching law at Pisa and later at Perugia. Susanne Lepsius, "Bartolus de Saxoferrato," in *CALMA: Compendium Auctorum Latinorum Medii Aevi (500-1500)*, ed. Michael Lapidge, Gian Carlo Garfagnini, and Claudio Leonardi, vol. 2.1 (Tavarnuzze: SISMEL edizioni del Galluzzo, 2004), 101–56.

[22] Covarrubias, *Commentary on Rule Possessor* 2.6.6.

of a third person, in which case you can proceed against him; see the provisions to this effect in Roman law.[23]

15. I think we need a clear distinction here. When the invincible mistake that was the cause that gave rise to the contract is laid bare, the case is either still intact or not. If it is still intact, you cannot be obliged to fulfill the contract before the tribunal of conscience, unless perhaps if you are forced by the verdict of a judge. This is evident in the case of betrothal. For a deceived person can no longer be held to fulfill his contract from the moment he discovers that something was kept hidden that, had he known about it from the beginning, would have prevented him from wanting to enter into the contract. However, if the case is no longer intact—for instance, if both or one of the parties fulfilled their contractual obligations—we have to make another distinction. For the party who was not deceived was either knowledgeable about the vice or defect or he was not. If he did not know, the laws do not permit rescinding the contract. They only grant the *actio quanti minoris*, the remedy of price reduction. This means that the price is reduced for the amount that you would not have paid should you have bought the good after the detection of the defect.[24] This does not only apply to contracts of buying and selling but also to barter.[25] But if the person who makes a contract with you does know of the defect beforehand, the contract may be rescinded at your option after it has been exposed.[26] The reason for this is that he is then considered to have been a participant in the deceit. For he was bound—at least according to positive law—to reveal all hidden defects to you, as is stated in Justinian's Digest.[27] If he failed to reveal

---

[23] Dig. 4.3.7; Dig. 50.14.2.
[24] Dig. 19.1.13.
[25] Dig. 21.1.19.
[26] Dig. 19.1.13.
[27] Dig. 21.1.1.

the hidden defects, he sinned against justice. See further Medina, *Codex on Restitution*.[28]

---

[28] Medina, *Codex on Restitution* 34. Ed. note: Juan de Medina (1490–1546) taught theology at the University of Alcalá de Henares. He wrote a treatise on penance, restitution, and contracts that was avidly cited by his colleagues in Salamanca and abroad. Medina was much more rigorous about the duty to reveal hidden defects than many of his colleagues in Salamanca or, for that matter, than the Jesuit contemporaries of Becanus. See Wim Decock and Jan Hallebeek, "Pre-Contractual Duties to Inform in Early Modern Scholasticism," *Tijdschrift voor Rechtsgeschiedenis/The Legal History Review* 78 (2010): 89–133 (108).

4

Under Which Circumstances Is a Promise under Oath Valid?

1. For a promise or contract under oath to carry obligatory force, two considerations have to be taken into account: one on the part of the promise, the other on the part of the oath. If the promise is valid by itself based on the grounds I stated before, it will become even more valid and firm when we add an oath to it. If, on the other hand, it is not valid by itself due to some defect, we need to resort to the oath and see whether this is valid in such a way that the promise, which otherwise would not be enforceable by itself, must still be performed because of the oath. In order to do this, we need to observe these two rules.

2. *The first rule.* When what is being promised to someone under oath can be done without any sin of the person who makes the promise, the oath is valid and has to be kept. That is to say, if the person to whose advantage the oath has been sworn wishes it to be kept, and there are no other grounds on which the oath can be lifted lawfully, the oath cannot be lifted lawfully. The reason for this rule is that honor of and regard for the Divine Majesty, upon whom we call as a witness when swearing an oath, demand we make sure whatever we promise is true, if at least this can be done licitly, lest we make him witness of falsehood.

3. *The second rule.* When the person who makes the promise under oath cannot do what he promises without commiting a sin, the oath is invalid and void. The reason is that no one can be obliged to sin; the opposite view would be contradictory.

4. Both rules can be easily derived from the canon law: "Oaths of this kind need to be kept"—namely, those sworn over a nonbinding contract according to civil law—"if they were made freely, without force or deceit, since they are not harmful to the other party and do not lead to the loss of eternal salvation when observed."[1] It follows *a contrario* that oaths should not be kept when this leads to the loss of salvation. This is the case when keeping the oath leads to mortal or venial sin. The same can be derived from the following rule of law in the *Liber Sextus*: "An oath going against good morals does not have obligatory force."[2] Beware: this rule concerns natural good morals, the opposite of which is sin; it does not concern civic good morals, which are put in place in a state only to make it a politically well-ordered one; see Sylvester.[3]

5. At this point one must carefully note that a promise must be fulfilled in a different way when the promise itself is valid and an oath is added to it from when the promise itself is invalid and an oath is added to it. For in the former case the promise has to be fulfilled both by force of the promise, which carries obligatory force by itself, and by force of the oath, which adds a new obligation; whereas in the latter, it needs to be fulfilled by force of the oath alone, not of the promise, which, after all, is invalid by itself. Because of that, in the

---

[1] Dec. Greg. 2.24.28. See also Liber Sextus 1.18.2.

[2] Liber Sextus 5, *De regulis iuris* 58.

[3] Sylvester, *Summa silvestrina*, s.v. "pactum," nos. 8 and 11. Ed. note: Silvester Mazzolini da Prierio (also known as Sylvester Prierias, 1456–1523) was a Dominican friar, theologian at the papal palace in Rome, and author of a widespread manual for confessors, the so-called *Summa silvestrina*. He played a seminal role in handing down the medieval tradition of penitential literature to the theologians and jurists belonging to the School of Salamanca. See Michael Tavuzzi, *Prierias: The Life and Works of Silvestro Mazzolini da Prierio* (Durham, NC: Duke University Press, 1997).

latter case you will be obliged to nothing if the oath is let go of, but in the former you will still be bound by the force of the promise, albeit not by that of the oath.

6. I shall clarify this with an example. Suppose you promised your friend one hundred golden coins, out of free will and accompanied with an oath, and he accepted your promise under oath. In that case you are bound by two titles, that of the promise and that of the oath. If the oath is let go of in a lawful way, you will still be bound by the promise. In contrast, if you promised a robber the same amount of money under pressure of violence or grave fear, and an oath came on top of this, you will be bound only by the title of the oath; after lawful relaxation of the oath, you will be freed from any obligation. The reason for this difference is that by means of the valid promise itself, you transfer the right to enforce the promise to the promisee, but not through an invalid promise. By analogy, we can say the same about a contract—that is, an onerous promise.

7. I need to explain here what I have said about the relaxation of an oath. In general, the obligation stemming from an oath may be lifted in two ways: first, by impeding it from coming into force in the first place; second, by lifting the obligation that has already been introduced. *With regard to the first way*, the obligation stemming from an oath can be impeded by law if the law clearly states that an oath added to a contract or promise is invalid and does not carry any obligation whatsoever. In this way, the Council of Trent declared an oath regarding renunciation of goods invalid if it was sworn prior to the two-month period preceding profession.[4] This was obviously done to meet and consider the freedom of the novices and to exclude any form of coercion. And similarly, in the kingdom of Portugal, any contract, obligation, agreement, promise, remission, or dissolution confirmed with an oath has been declared invalid by law if their judicial examination would otherwise have been a matter for the secular court, unless the oath has been added with royal permission. It is almost the same in the kingdom of Castile, with the exception of certain contracts,

---

[4] Council of Trent, session 25, decree 7 (on regulars and nuns), chapter 16.

as Molina writes.[5] This was done to prevent people from bringing disputes over this type of contract before an ecclesiastical court. For an oath makes a case that otherwise would merely be civil, a matter of both courts.[6]

8. *Objections.* How could it be possible for a law or human power to obstruct the obligation of an oath since this obligation naturally and necessarily results from the oath? For it is by natural law that we are obliged not to make God witness of falsehood. *My answer:* This is possible in two ways. First, if a human law makes the person to whose favor the oath of the promise has been sworn incapable of accepting it. For it is evident that this oath has no obligatory force unless the promise is accepted by the promisee, and if he is not capable of accepting it, no obligation can originate at all. It is certain that civil law can institute such an incapacity because it can declare someone incapable of taking on certain offices, of contracts, alienations, of acquiring goods, and the like—so why not of validly accepting the promise of someone else? Second, it is also possible when a prince, through a law he himself issues, releases the promisor from his obligation by the mere fact that he tries to create it. For if a private person to whose favor a promise has been sworn may immediately release the promisor from this obligation and wave his own right to enforce it, why would a prince not be able to do so? The prince is superior to that private person, so why would he not be able, in the name of his subject, to release the promisor from his obligation for a just cause?

9. I will now move on to *the second way* of lifting the obligation resulting from an oath. The obligation of an oath that already has been sworn may be lifted in various ways. First, when the subject of the oath changes, and as a result, what has been sworn becomes impossible or even illicit for the person who took the oath. Second, in case of a debt cancellation, for instance when the person to whose favor the oath has been made releases the promisor from the obligation. Third, in case of a substitution, as when the person to whom the oath has been made grants that something else may be performed instead of the service

---

[5] Molina, *On Justice and Right* 2.149.

[6] As is obvious from Liber Sextus 2.2.3.

promised under oath. Fourth, in case of an invalidation, as when the subject of the promissory oath turns out to be in someone else's power. Fifth, in case of dispensation—for instance, when someone higher in power grants you a dispensation so that you will not be bound to keep the promise to someone else you had made under oath. However, the superior cannot do this without a legitimate cause because it is not possible to take away someone else's right without a just cause. The following causes are just: (1) if the oath originated through fear or fraud; (2) if some other injustice intervened—for example, when a usurious money lender requires the debtor to swear an oath to pay interest; (3) by way of a just punishment; (4) if the common good requires so, as when you promise under oath not to accuse someone. See St. Thomas,[7] Pedro de Aragón,[8] and Sylvester.[9]

10. *You may object*: How can a superior use dispensatory power over an oath? For even though a prince may, through his own legislation, somehow prevent an obligation to originate from an oath, as has been said before, he does not seem to be able to lift an obligation when it has already come into force. That would, after all, be nothing else than granting a dispensation for committing perjury after already having confirmed something under oath and for making God witness of falsehood. *I answer*: two different things are at stake here. It is something different to directly lift the obligation of an oath that has just been introduced from laying down or lifting something through the effects of which the obligation ceases spontaneously. A superior cannot do the former; the latter cannot be performed only by a supe-

---

[7] Thomas Aquinas, *Summa theologiae* II.2, Q. 89, A. 7 and 9.

[8] Pedro de Aragón, *Commentaries on the Secunda Secundae about Justice and Right*, II.2, Q. 89, A. 7 and 9. Ed. note: Pedro de Aragón (also known as Petrus Aragonensis, c. 1545–1592) belonged to the order of the Augustinians in Salamanca, where he taught theology and occupied the chair of Scotist philosophy for a while. See Theodore Tack, *Fray Pedro de Aragón O.S.A.: His Life, Works and Doctrine on Restitution* (Chicago: Augustinian Press, 1957). His commentary on Thomas Aquinas's *Summa theologiae* was popular among the Jesuits.

[9] Sylvester, *Summa silvestrina*, s.v. "iuramentum," no. 5 and elsewhere.

rior, but even by others. Here we need to take notice that, in the case of a promissory oath, there are some tacit and implicit conditions. If they are added or taken away, the obligation of the oath ceases by itself without any risk of perjury. I am speaking of these and similar conditions: "I promise and swear I will perform this for you"—that is to say, *if you want it and unless you release me from the obligation; if a competent superior does not contradict it; or, unless the superior releases me from the obligation through his authority*. If one of these conditions is added or taken away—like when you release me from what I promised or when a superior contradicts the obligation or releases you from it—the obligation of the oath ceases to exist.

5

WHERE DOES THE OBLIGATION OF A VALID PROMISE COME FROM?

1. Following the three types of promise—namely, the gratuitous promise, the onerous promise, and the promise under oath, which I have dealt with before—I will draw three conclusions. *The first conclusion.* The obligation, which holds one to a gratuitous and free promise, stems from two virtues, truth and faith. Hence, if a person does not do what he promised, he commits sin in two ways: (1) being a liar, going against the virtue of truth; (2) being perfidious and faithless, going against the virtue of faith or fidelity.

2. *The second conclusion.* The obligation, which holds one to what he promised in an onerous contract, stems from three virtues—namely, truth, fidelity, and justice. And if one does not do what he promised, he commits sin in three ways: (1) being a liar, (2) being perfidious or faithless, and (3) being unjust.

3. *The third conclusion.* The obligation that holds one to what he promised under oath does not stem only from the virtues mentioned above but also from the virtue of religion. Hence, if the promise was gratuitous and an oath comes on top of it, one is bound by three virtues: those of truth, fidelity, and religion; if it was onerous, by four

virtues: truth, fidelity, justice, and religion. And if he does not keep his promise, he is lying, faithless, unjust, and perjurious.

4. This, however, has been said in general. Now we must explain each virtue and its resulting obligations individually. To start off, the *virtue of truth* obliges us to two things: (1) to make our promises sincerely, not fictitiously, which means our intention should agree with what we promise in words; (2) to make sure we do in reality what we promised. Scholastics explain it in these terms: *to align our words with our intentions and our deeds with our words*. Both requirements are to be met in order to be truthful in speaking or promising, as Cajetan teaches us.[1] We can also find this in St. Thomas.[2]

5. The *virtue of faith*, or fidelity, obliges us to one thing: to make sure we do what we promised. And even though this obligation seems to be the same as the previous one, that of truth, it is nevertheless different. First, because the obligation of truth has a much wider scope than that of fidelity. The latter applies only to the affirmation of a promise, whereas the former also applies to affirmations without promises.[3] Second, the obligation of fidelity is stronger than that of truth. Someone who promises he will do something is bound by a stronger obligation than someone who simply affirms this without making a promise. For someone who only affirms is liable to do what he said by merely one title—namely, by virtue of the prohibition on being mendacious in his words. But someone who made a promise lays under the obligation of two titles: not to be mendacious in his words but also not to violate someone else's right to the thing that has been promised. The reason

---

[1] Cajetan, *Commentaries on the Secunda Secundae* Q. 113, A. 1, just before the end. Ed. note: Tommaso de Vio (1469–1534) was a theologian belonging to the Dominican order. He is better known as Cardinal Cajetan, a name which he derived from his birthplace, Gaeta, and his appointment as cardinal by Pope Leo X. Cajetan is famous for his commentary on Thomas's *Summa theologiae*. It was avidly consulted by theologians and jurists of the School of Salamanca. Cajetan's commentary on Thomas has been included in the standard edition of Thomas Aquinas's work commissioned by Pope Leo XIII.

[2] Thomas Aquinas, *Summa theologiae* II.2, Q. 80, A. 1 ad 3.

[3] Thomas Aquinas, *Summa theologiae* II.2, Q. 80, A. 1 ad 3.

for this is that a promiser not only puts himself under the obligation to refrain from lying but also grants another person the right to claim what has been promised.

6. The *virtue of justice*, which applies in contracts or onerous promises, obliges us to give everyone his due by virtue of the contract. That explains the general definition of justice given by the Roman jurist Ulpian: "Justice is the firm and perpetual will to give everyone his rightful due."[4] We can find similar definitions with St. Augustine,[5] St. Ambrose,[6] St. Thomas,[7] and other authors in various passages.

7. The *virtue of religion* obliges us to display reverence and due adoration of God, as St. Thomas teaches us.[8] This, however, may be done in different ways. One example, which we are discussing here, is through an oath. The oath is in fact an outward adoration through which we profess that God is of infallible truth, and we call upon him to witness that we speak the truth. Accordingly, if someone misuses this adoration and makes God witness of falsehood, whereas he needed to invoke him as the witness of truth, he goes against the obligation of the virtue of religion and commits perjury.

This was a brief overview of the obligatory force of the virtues that apply to promises and pacts. Now we must consider the strength of this obligation.

---

[4] Dig. 1.1.10*pr.*

[5] Augustine, *City of God* 19.21.

[6] Ambrose, *On Duties* 1.24.

[7] Thomas Aquinas, *Summa theologiae* II.2, Q. 58.

[8] Thomas Aquinas, *Summa theologiae* II.2, Q. 81, A. 2.

6

How Strong Is the Obligation of a Valid Promise?

1. In the previous chapter I explained how this obligation takes its origin from different virtues—namely, truth, fidelity, justice, and religion. To determine how strong this obligation is, it is therefore necessary to unfold how strong the obligation of the virtues mentioned is. And because there are four virtues, I will draw the same number of conclusions.

2. *The first conclusion.* The virtue of truth, which obliges you to promise sincerely and do what you promised lest you become a liar, is always binding on pain of sin. By itself it is only binding on pain of venial sin, but it may also bind on pain of mortal sin because of an accidental circumstance, such as damage or injustice. The reason for this is that a lie is always a sin and that if the lie does not harm anyone, it is only a venial sin; however, should the lie result in serious harm, it may even constitute a mortal sin, according to St. Thomas.[1] He distinguishes three types of lies: the humorous, the useful, and the pernicious. He says the first two are venial sins, whereas the third and last one is mortal. We speak of a humorous lie when it is brought

---

[1] Thomas Aquinas, *Summa theologiae* II.2, Q. 110, A. 2 and 4.

up only as a joke or for entertainment purposes, of a useful lie when it benefits someone, and of a pernicious one when it unjustly harms someone. But, in fact, a lie may be pernicious in two different ways. First, when it is harmful to God. This is the case in matters of faith, during the sacrament of confession, and under oath. Second, when it is harmful to a neighbor, as applies in case of slander, false testimony, and unfair contracts.

3. For a better understanding of this conclusion, we need to unfold and examine each part of it separately. We may ask (1) whether any lie is a sin, (2) whether it is a sin by its own nature or merely on account of prohibition, (3) whether it is so sinful that it is licit on no occasion whatsoever, and (4) whether some lies are greater sins than others.

4. With regard to *the first question*: Catholics teach that every lie is a sin. The reason for this is clear: everything God prohibits and condemns is a sin, and he prohibits and condemns every lie. The biblical evidence is abundant: "You shall not deal falsely; you shall not lie to one another" (Lev. 19:11); "You destroy those who speak lies" (Ps. 5:7); "There are six things that the Lord hates, seven that are an abomination to Him: haughty eyes, a lying tongue" (Prov. 6:16); "The righteous hates falsehood" (Prov. 13:5); "A mouth that lies, kills the soul" (Wis. 1:11); "Be not willing to make any manner of lie" (Sir. 7:14); "Therefore, having put away falsehood, let each one of you speak the truth with his neighbor, for we are members of one another" (Eph. 4:25); "Do not lie to one another" (Col. 3:9).

5. From these and similar sources, we can be sure every lie is prohibited, and accordingly, it cannot be said without sin. Now we can move on to the *second question*, whether it is a sin by its own nature, like adultery, blasphemy, hatred of God, or merely on account of prohibition, like eating the fruit in Paradise. Theologians agree it is a sin by its own nature. A lie naturally contains a threefold deformity or evil against right reason: the misuse of speech, the deception of our neighbor, and the violation of human friendship. Someone who lies, first, makes misuse of speech, since nature has given man the use of language and speech so that he can manifest his own internal, hidden conceptions to others. But through a lie, the exact opposite takes place. In this way our neighbor is deceived. For when you think one thing but

say another, your neighbor, expecting you to speak honestly, acquires a false impression. He, after all, believes you mean what you say, but you do the opposite. Consequently, you commit a grave violation of the natural law of friendship because you do unto someone else what you would not want to happen to yourself, which goes against charity. This is more or less the reasoning Augustine follows in his *Enchiridion*: "Every lie must be called a sin because a man must say what he carries in his heart. A person who lies speaks against the feelings in his heart. And undoubtedly, speech was introduced not to make people deceive one another, but for each person to make his or her thoughts known to the other. So to use words for deceit, not for what they were intended for, is a sin."[2]

6. Augustine makes the same argument in his book on lying to Consentius on the basis of this passage in the First Letter of John: "because a lie can never be based on the truth" (2:21). Starting off at this point, his argumentation goes as follows: someone who says lying is licit either teaches the truth or an untruth. If he teaches an untruth, we should not believe him; if he teaches the truth, also some lie must be of the truth, which goes against the apostle. These are Augustine's own words:

> I know that even a person who teaches that one should lie wants us to believe he teaches the truth. Because if his teachings are untrue, who would like to study a false doctrine, in which the teacher deceives and the student is deceived? However, if in order to attract a student he maintains that he teaches the truth while teaching one should lie, how will there be any lie based on the truth, when John the apostle clearly contradicts this by saying that a lie can never be based on the truth? Therefore, it is not true that one should sometimes lie. And what is not true should never be recommended to anyone.[3]

---

[2] Augustine, *Enchiridion (On Faith, Hope and Love)* 7.22.

[3] Augustine, *On Lying (to Consentius)* 18.

Somewhat further he writes:

> Whoever speaks against me to persuade and defend a single lie—what does he say after all if he does not speak the truth? If we must listen to him because he speaks the truth, how does he want me to become a liar by telling the truth? How can a lie take the truth as its advocate? Or does the lie try to win for its opponent, truth, just to be defeated by it shortly after? Who would come up with such absurdities? Therefore, let us never say that those who assert one should sometimes lie are truthful while asserting this, lest we believe—what would be most absurd and foolish—that the truth should teach us to be liars. No one learns to commit adultery from chastity, no one learns to offend God from piety, no one learns to hurt another from friendliness—but we should learn to lie from truth? What is more, if truth does not teach this, it is not true; if it is not true, we ought not to learn it; and if we ought not to learn it, we must never lie.[4]

Thus Augustine.

7. The following words about the devil in the gospel of John point in the same direction: "When he lies, he speaks out of his own character, for he is a liar and the father of lies" (John 8:44). From this passage I draw the following conclusion. Something of which the devil is the first author and inventor cannot be anything else but evil, when on the other hand God is the Father of every good. The devil is the father and inventor of the lie. Therefore, a lie cannot be anything but evil. The minor premise is clear from the passage quoted: "When he lies, he speaks out of his own character"[5]—that is to say, he uses his own[6] invention and malice. For no one taught him to lie, but he taught others by his own example, for instance, when he spoke in Paradise, "You

---

[4] Augustine, *On Lying (to Consentius)* 19.

[5] *ex propriis.*

[6] *propria.*

will not surely die."[7] So he is a liar and the father of the lie. Augustine expresses this elegantly in his commentary on John: "Just like God the Father begot his Son, the Truth, the devil begot Lie as a bastard son."[8]

8. My *third question* was whether a lie is such a great sin that it is allowed on no occasion whatsoever, not even if you were to hurt no one but rather help someone by lying, to preserve life, chastity, good name, or health or to avoid another great evil. This question has been there since antiquity. Plato, the Priscillianists, Origen, and Cassian thought it was licit. On the contrary, all theologians and orthodox fathers deny this. St. Augustine brings up the question in chapter 13 of his *Enchiridion* and finally provides us with an answer in chapter 22:

> We must not think a lie is no sin because we may sometimes benefit someone by lying. We may also benefit someone by stealing if the poor person we publicly offer it greatly profits from it, and the rich person we secretly take it away from does not even notice it. But still, no one would say such a theft is no sin. We may be of benefit to someone by committing adultery, too, if a woman appears to die from love if we do not abide by her wishes and if she were to live she would purify herself by repentance. Still, such adultery is a sin. So if we rightly appreciate chastity, why have we taken offense at truth, so that we are not willing to violate the former for someone else's sake by committing adultery but are ready to violate the latter by lying? Lying cannot be praised because sometimes we lie for the good of some people.[9]

9. Augustine discusses this question more elaborately in his book on lying. After having shown various examples from Scripture, defending

---

[7] Ed. note: Gen. 3:4.

[8] Augustine, *Tractates on the Gospel of John* 42.

[9] Augustine, *Enchiridion (On Faith, Hope and Love)* 7.22. Ed. note: The final sentence appears in italics in Becanus's Latin text, which erroneously suggests that the sentence is still part of the quotation from Augustine. Becanus, like other early modern authors, may have used an edition of Augustine's *Enchiridion* that was corrupt.

both sides of the argument, he concludes in the last chapter, "Now that we have discussed everything, it is clear that these testimonies from the Scriptures only teach us one should never lie at all."[10] Further on he adds, "Whoever thinks there is some type of lie which is not a sin will deceive himself shamefully, for he believes he—a deceiver of others—is an honest man."[11]

10. Theologians present a most effective argument for this proposition in the following manner. Things that are intrinsically and naturally evil and illicit can never become good and licit, not even when they are done for a good cause; a lie is intrinsically and naturally evil, as I have proved before. Therefore, a lie can never become good and licit, no matter the cause it is made for. The major of this syllogism is evident because what is intrinsically and naturally evil cannot become good by any extrinsic circumstance whatsoever. Extrinsic and accidental circumstances do not change the nature and intrinsic essence of the thing. As Augustine rightly wrote in his book against lying, "It matters enormously for what reason, to which end, and with what intention something is being done. Those things we know for sure to be sins must never be done—not under the pretext of a good reason, not to a so-called good end, not as if it were with good intention."[12]

11. The apostle Paul spoke in this sense in his letter to the Romans: "It is not allowed to do evil that good may come of it" (3:8). Why? Because what is evil by itself does not become licit through the intention of a good end. Based on the same argument, Augustine shows in his book against lying that it is not licit to lie when we try to convert heretics. He says, "So how could I rightly prosecute lies with a lie? Or do you think we should prosecute theft with theft, sacrilege with sacrilege, adultery with adultery? But if the truth of God abounds by my lie, should we then not also say 'Let us do evil, so that good things may come'? No—behold how much the apostle hates this. What is the difference after all between 'Let us lie to guide heretic liars toward the

---

[10] Augustine, *On Lying (to Consentius)* 21.42.

[11] Ed. note: Augustine, *On Lying (to Consentius)* 21.42.

[12] Augustine, *Against Lying* 7.18.

truth,' and 'Let us do evil, so that good things may come'?"[13] Later on, in chapter 7, Augustine writes, "If lies are just because they are made with the intention to detect latent heretics, even adultery can be chaste when committed with the same intention."[14] And below in the same chapter, "Who would say, so that we have something to give to the poor, 'Let us steal from the rich' or 'Let us sell false testimonies'?"[15] And again in the same place: "Who could say such things unless someone wanted to try to subvert human society, all morals, and laws? Of which most horrendous crime, which most scandalous deed, which most impious sacrilege could it not be said that it is possible to be done rightly or justly, once we will have conceded that in all evil acts of men we should not inquire about what is happening; and this, for the reason that whatever acts are found to have been done for good reasons should not even be judged evil?" These and more examples are given by Augustine.

12. The *fourth question* is whether all lies are equally serious sins. Catholics deny this along with Augustine, who writes in his *Enchiridion*, "To me it seems every lie is a sin, but it does make a huge difference with which intention and about which affairs someone is lying. A person who tells a lie to be helpful does not sin in the same way as someone who lies with the desire to do harm. And someone who sends a traveler in the wrong direction by lying does not cause as much harm as the person who depraves our way of life with deceiving lies."[16] In the same book, after having said every lie is a sin, even the one made for the salvation of others, he adds about this last type of lie, "To conclude, it is a sin, but only a venial one; the goodwill pardons, the deceit renders guilty."[17] The argument Augustine makes is clear: someone

---

[13] Augustine, *Against Lying* 1.1.

[14] Augustine, *Against Lying* 7.17.

[15] Augustine, *Against Lying* 7.18.

[16] Augustine, *Enchiridion (On Faith, Hope and Love)* 6.18. Ed. note: There are some passages missing in the Latin text quoted by Becanus in comparison with the text in the modern standard edition by Migne (PL 40).

[17] Augustine, *Enchiridion (On Faith, Hope and Love)* 7.22. Ed. note: The quote does not correspond to the Latin text in the Migne edition (PL 40).

who inflicts harm by lying commits a greater sin than someone who does no harm, but rather helps.

13. I have spoken sufficiently about the obligation of truth and the disapproval of lies. Now I shall deal with the obligation of the other virtues—namely, fidelity, justice, and religion—but much more succinctly and compendiously. For once it has been settled that truth obliges at all time at the risk of sin in such a way that lying is never allowed, it is evident that fidelity, justice, and religion always oblige as well, in such a way that to be perfidious, unjust, or sacrilegious is never allowed. In fact, these virtues impose a greater obligation than truth, and violating them makes for a greater wrongdoing than a mere and simple lie. Let us therefore move on to the second conclusion.

14. *The second conclusion.* The virtue of fidelity, which holds you to keep your promise lest you become unfaithful and perfidious, obliges by itself on pain of mortal sin, unless the insignificance of the substance involved pleads as an excuse. We can find this in Dr. Navarrus,[18] Soto,[19] Richard,[20] Antonine of Florence,[21] and Sylvester.[22] At this

---

But the meaning of Becanus's quotation corresponds to the relevant passage in the *Enchiridion*, and the Latin text he quotes widely circulated among early modern authors.

[18] Dr. Navarrus, *Enchiridion or Manual for Confessors and Penitents* 18.6.

[19] Soto, *On Justice and Right* 7.2.1 ad 1.

[20] Richard, *On the Sentences* 4.38.3.3. Ed. note: Richard de Mediavilla, or Richard of Middleton (c. 1249–c. 1308), was a Franciscan theologian in Paris. Middleton's commentary on Peter Lombard's *Sentences* remained popular among early modern scholastics. Richard Cross, "Richard of Middleton," in *Encyclopedia of Medieval Philosophy*, ed. Henrik Lagerlund (Dordrecht: Springer, 2011), 1:1132–34.

[21] Antonine of Florence, *Summa of Moral Theology* 2.20.1.4. Ed. note: Antonine of Florence (1389–1459), a Dominican friar, gained great fame as archbishop of Florence. He was the author of several books on confessional practice that were still used in the School of Salamanca. See Kerstin Schlögl-Flierl, *Moraltheologie für den Alltag. Eine moraltheologische Untersuchung der Bussbücher des Antonius von Florenz OP* (Münster: Aschendorff, 2017).

[22] Sylvester, *Summa silvestrina*, s.v. "pactum," no. 4.

point I would like to state again what I already mentioned before: it entails more to promise something than to merely affirm it. For someone who promises another person he will give him something does not only affirm he will do so but also obligates himself toward the other and consequently grants him the right to demand what has been promised. This right is being violated when the promiser does not keep his faith. So here is the first proof for the second conclusion: violating someone else's right in a weighty matter is a mortal sin, which speaks for itself; the virtue of fidelity obliges us not to violate the right of the other person to the thing that has been promised; consequently, in a weighty matter, this is an obligation on pain of mortal sin.

15. Second, the conclusion is proved because the obligation fidelity puts on the promiser is so serious it could even lead to a case in public court, and the promiser may be compelled to fulfill his promise, especially when the specific formula of a stipulation has been added. This point is generally accepted. Thus we are dealing with a strict obligation, which places us in a weighty matter at the risk of mortal sin. *Objection*: A promise by itself does not carry so much weight that it may lead to a case in public court; this only happens on the basis of the added formula of stipulation. *My answer*: This formula does not make a promise stronger before the tribunal of conscience, but merely in public court, because the stipulation creates the presumption that the promise has been made with more deliberation. Moreover, even though according to the law of the Digest a stipulation is required to make a promise enforceable in the external court, it does not seem to be required according to the law of the Code.[23] Neither is it required in the kingdom of Castile, as Molina notes.[24] Lastly, regardless of what civil law has to say about it, granting an *actio* on the ground of an accepted promise is allowed under canon law, even if no formula of stipulation has been made. This can be deduced from canon *Antigonus*[25] and is the

---

[23] As most legal scholars derive from Cod. 8.53.35*pr*.

[24] Molina, *On Justice and Right* 2.254.

[25] Dec. Greg. 1.35.1.

common opinion among the experts, as Gómez[26] and Covarrubias[27] both testify. And it is of no importance that canon law requires the expression of a reason.[28] Canon law requires that because when you do not express a reason why you make a promise, your promise seems to be motivated by mistake. However, this presumption ceases before the tribunal of conscience; see Sylvester[29] and Dr. Navarrus.[30]

16. Third, this conclusion is proved by the testimony of Christ, who explicitly teaches that the precept of fidelity is among the weightier rules of divine law. In fact, he says in the gospel of Matthew, "Woe to you, scribes and Pharisees, hypocrites! For you tithe mint and dill and cumin, and have neglected the weightier matters of the law: justice and mercy and faithfulness" (23:23). By "faithfulness" here he means fidelity in honoring agreements. He says this belongs to the weightier matters prescribed by the law. And that is true. According to the old law, those precepts whose transgression needed to be atoned for with a sacrifice were seen as being more important, and the precept of fidelity in keeping agreements is one of them. We can find evidence of this in the book of Leviticus: "Anyone who commited a sin and, contemptuous of God, failed to return a deposit to his neighbor—a deposit that was committed to his faithfulness—shall restore it in full and sacrifice an immaculate ram from his herd" (6:2).[31] This is why Christ says, "Woe to you, scribes and Pharisees." He even adds the reason for it: "for you have neglected faithfulness." And certainly

---

[26] Gómez, *Commentaries and Various Resolutions* 2.9.2.

[27] Covarrubias, *Relection on canon* Quamvis pactum 2.4.14 and 15.

[28] *causa*. Ed. note: In the early modern scholastic tradition, this notion is primarily used to indicate the absence or presence of a mistake in the formation of the contract. See Wim Decock, *Theologians and Contract Law: The Moral Transformation of the* Ius Commune *(ca. 1500–1650)* (Leiden: Brill, 2013), 135, 149–50, 611, including a discussion of Sylvester's and Dr. Navarrus's positions.

[29] Sylvester, *Summa silvestrina*, s.v. "pactum," no. 3.

[30] Dr. Navarrus, *Enchiridion or Manual for Confessors and Penitents*, 18.6.

[31] Ed. note: The quotation is imprecise and includes part of v. 6.

when Christ threatens someone with a "woe," this is a clear sign the person has committed a grave crime.

17. In the fourth place, our conclusion is proved by its effect. Because from faithfully keeping one's contracts, the regard of both God and our fellow men follows, as well as the glory and greatness of one's name, the security of the people, tranquility of the republic, and unharmed treatises of war and peace. From faithlessness the exact opposite follows. Pedro de Ribadeneira explains this thoroughly.[32] Lipsius also illustrates this point with brilliant examples.[33] And let us read history. How often do we not find, as a pejorative remark, "Punic faithfulness," "Greek faithfulness," "the ever mendacious Cretans"? How often, conversely, do we not find with great approbation, "said and done"; "the word of a king carries his seal"; "with Germanic faith and steadiness"; "written in Jupiter's tables"—and suchlike phrases?

18. *The third conclusion.* The virtue of justice, through which we are bound to keep our promises in onerous pacts and contracts, always obliges us on pain of mortal sin, unless the insignificance of the matter pleads as an excuse. Theologians assert this at various places alongside St. Thomas.[34] The reason behind this is that justice compels us to grant to another what is due to him by law, following the well-known maxim of Ulpian: "Justice is the firm and perpetual will to give everyone his rightful due."[35] Not granting another person what law entitles him to is a mortal sin in a weighty matter because it is plain injustice, which is loathed in various passages in the Bible—for example, Psalm 5:6: "The boastful shall not stand before your eyes"; and Psalm 36:28: "The unjust shall be punished, and the seed of the wicked shall perish." In Deuteronomy 25:16 we find, "For all who do such things, all who pervert justice, are an abomination to the Lord your God." Among all nations, those who commit injustice are severely punished, such

---

[32] Ribadeneira, *The Christian Prince* 2.15.

[33] Lipsius, *Political Admonitions and Examples* 2.13.

[34] Thomas Aquinas, *Summa theologiae* II.2, Q. 59, A. 4.

[35] Ed. note: Dig. 1.1.10*pr.*

as thieves, murderers, robbers, false witnesses, corrupt judges, and those kinds of wicked people.

19. Even though the obligation of justice is similar to that of fidelity—both bind us not to violate the right of another person—it is still profoundly different and even much more important. This is because a right is stronger when it stems from an onerous contract rather than from a simple promise. (1) A promise may be revoked more easily than a contract. (2) A promise grants only a distant right to the thing that has been promised. (3) If a promiser does not keep his promise, he cannot be held to compensate for lost profits,[36] but someone who signs a contract and violates it will be bound to do so. (4) A promise does not forbid that, later, the thing promised is said to be given freely; a contract, however, forbids a free donation. (5) It is regarded a greater injustice if someone refuses to pay off one hundred golden coins due to be paid by virtue of a contract than if they were due to be paid only on the basis of a voluntary promise.

20. *The fourth conclusion.* The virtue of religion, by which you are bound to keep a promise or an agreement performed under oath lest you commit perjury, puts you under obligation at the risk of mortal sin, for perjury is a mortal sin and an extremely heavy one indeed, as all theologians acknowledge with St. Thomas.[37] The reason for this is that someone who swears falsely makes God assent to an untruth, to the extent he is capable to do so, which is a horrible form of injustice. This is why the most serious punishments have been imposed upon the perjured. Among the Scythians and the Egyptians, they were beheaded. Among the Indians, their hands and feet were cut off. According to civil law, those who have committed perjury and hereby damaged another are called infamous.[38] In canon law they are called infamous too, at least if the affair is notorious;[39] see also Covarrubias.[40]

---

[36] *lucrum cessans.*

[37] Thomas Aquinas, *Summa theologiae* II.2, Q. 98, A. 3.

[38] Gloss on Cod. 2.4.41*pr.*

[39] Dec. Grat. C.6 q.1 c.2 and c.18.

[40] Covarrubias, *Relection on canon* Quamvis pactum 1.7.2.

21. From everything I have said here it has become clear how strong the obligation of a promise really is. For if the promise is gratuitous, it binds us by two titles; if it is onerous, by three; and if it is made under oath, by four. And, except for one, each of these obligations is most of the time binding on pain of mortal sin. Let us now move on to the main question.

7

Do We Have to Keep Our Faith with Heretics in the Case of a Valid Promise with Obligatory Force?

1. Up to this point I have shown what constitutes a valid promise and how strong its obligation is. Now I will examine the question whether a promise that is otherwise valid and carries obligatory force ceases to oblige for this one reason: that it has been made to a heretic. And consequently, whether you are bound to fulfill the promise you made to a heretic.

2. Following the judgment of theologians and canonists, I assume there are some cases in which a promise that would otherwise be valid ceases to oblige: First, if the thing promised becomes illicit or useless or impossible. Second, if the state of the things or persons involved changes so much that the promiser, according to the judgment of prudent men, does not seem to understand he wanted this particular outcome. This has to be judged on the basis of the condition of the thing promised, the promise itself, the disposition of the promisee, and other circumstances. Third, when two people made each other a promise, and one of them does not want to fulfill it.[1] Then the other

---

[1] Ed. note: The 1614 edition reads *impedire promissum*. We follow the 1607 edition, which reads *implere promissum*.

is not bound to fulfill the promise, but he may use a compensation. Here the old saying applies, "With the breaker of faith, faith may be broken."[2] Fourth, when something has been promised for an underlying reason that turns out not to exist—for instance, when you made a promise because you thought you would get a certain benefit from it, but you did not.[3] Then you are not bound to fulfill your promise; see St. Thomas,[4] Cajetan,[5] Dr. Navarrus,[6] and others. In these and similar cases, a promise that would otherwise be valid ceases to oblige, no matter whether it has been made to Catholics or to heretics.

3. But now the whole difficulty is to know whether, apart from these cases, a promise ceases to oblige when it has been made to heretics. Or do we need to add another category apart from the cases already mentioned—namely, heresy? Catholics teach two things about this. First, that we should not easily make promises to heretics. Second, that if a promise has been made, we should keep it nevertheless. I will briefly explain this in two conclusions.

4. *The first conclusion.* One should not easily enter into contracts, bargains, treaties, or agreements, whether public or private, with her-

---

[2] *Frangenti fidem, fides frangatur eidem.* Ed note: This rule, which reaches back to medieval canon law (e.g., Liber Sextus reg. iur. 75), is currently known in most legal systems as the *exceptio non adimpleti contractus,* or the "exception of non-performance." See James Crawford and Simon Olleson, "The Exception of Non-Performance: Links between the Law of Treaties and the Law of State Responsibility," *Australian Yearbook of International Law* 21 (2000): 55.

[3] Ed. note: This rule is commonly associated with the Roman *condictio causa data causa non secuta.* See James Gordley, *The Philosophical Origins of Modern Contract Doctrine* (Oxford: Clarendon Press, 1991), 53. Becanus refers to the transformation of this specific legal remedy into a general principle among scholastic theologians and canonists (see references below).

[4] Thomas Aquinas, *Summa theologiae* II.2, Q. 110, A. 3, ad 5.

[5] Cajetan, *Commentaries on the Secunda Secundae* Q. 113, A. 1, near the end.

[6] Dr. Navarrus, *Enchiridion or Manual for Confessors and Penitents* 18.7.

etics, chiefly for three reasons: (1) because of the danger of subversion, (2) because of the scandal involved, and (3) because of their depravity.

5. On the danger of subversion, we can generally look at what Ecclesiasticus has to say about that: "He who touches pitch shall be defiled with it; and he who has fellowship with the proud shall put on pride" (Sir. 13:1), which is especially true of the pride of heretics. More specific is Paul's second letter to Timothy: "and their talk will spread like gangrene" (2:17). Here he speaks about heretics who, as he says, subverted the faith of certain people. The reason is that heresy is similar to a contagious disease: just as no prudent person would quickly approach someone with a contagious disease so as not to endanger his bodily health, likewise no prudent person should easily deal with a heretic so as not to put the salvation of his soul at risk. For this reason God forbade the Jews in the Old Testament to enter into treaties, alliances, and friendships with pagans, lest they would turn away from the true belief in God by meeting them and would start to worship idols. We can read this in Exodus: "Take care, lest you make friendship with the inhabitants of the land to which you go, lest that becomes your ruin. You shall tear down their altars and break their statues and cut down their sacred poles (for you shall worship no other god, for the Lord, whose name is Jealous, is a jealous God), lest you make an agreement with the inhabitants of those lands and take of their daughters as brides for your sons; they will turn your sons into prostitutes for their gods" (34:12).[7] And in Deuteronomy: "You shall make no agreement with them. You shall not intermarry with them, giving your daughters to their sons or taking their daughters for your sons, for they would turn away your sons from following me to serve foreign gods more than me" (7:3).[8] And in other places we find similar passages. What is more, not only the ancient Jews, who for the most part were perverted by pagans a long time ago, testify how great this danger is and how harmful the contagion but also those Christians who lost their faith and salvation. We also learn it from daily experience because many people in almost every direction, especially

---

[7] Ed. note: The quotation extends through v. 16.

[8] Ed. note: The quotation includes part of v. 4.

in Germany, France, Belgium, and its neighboring provinces, left the Catholic Church and followed Calvin and Luther.

6. When it comes to the scandal involved, the case is equally clear. It is well known that many uneducated and simple folks suffer from this scandal and are misled when they see that their princes, noblemen, mighty, or learned meet heretics and bargain, enter into marriages, celebrate baptisms, and do similar things with them. They may think that they approve of the doctrine and morals of heretics because of this social intercourse, and from this they may start to believe they cannot be mistaken themselves if they follow their example. And so, little by little, they openly start to accept and defend heresy instead of the true doctrine, using no other argument than the belief that such people could not be mistaken and they can follow in their footsteps with a clear conscience. Nothing is more common in Germany and its neighboring territories. If only we had more people like Eleazar, who rather died than bring about a scandal. These words of his are crystal clear: "Such pretence is not worthy of a man of my age. Many of the young would suppose that Eleazar, in his ninetieth year, had gone over to an alien religion. Through my pretence, for the sake of living this miserable life a brief moment longer, they would be deceived while I defile and disgrace my old age" (2 Macc. 6:24–25). And the apostle says of himself, "Therefore, if food makes my brother stumble, I will never eat meat, lest I give scandal to my brother" (1 Cor. 8:13).

7. The apostle bears witness to the depravity of heretics: "For people will be lovers of self, lovers of money, proud, arrogant, blasphemous, disobedient to their parents, ungrateful, unholy, heartless, unappeasable, slanderous, without self-control, brutal, not loving the good, treacherous, reckless, swollen with conceit, lovers of pleasure rather than lovers of God, having the appearance of virtue and piety, but denying its power" (2 Tim. 3:2).[9] Consider how many and how grave the crimes of the heretics. Do you believe that people who are full of these depravities will keep their faith? I do not think so. That is why Paul adds, "Avoid such people."

---

[9] Ed. note: The quotation extends into v. 5.

8. *The second conclusion.* Even though you should not readily bargain with heretics, as has been made clear, you must nevertheless, once you have entered into an agreement or treaty with them and there is no objection other than the heresy, keep your faith with them sincerely and honestly, in no way less than to Catholics. The reason for this can be found in what I have said before. For the virtues that are at the origin of the obligation to keep our faith in promises oblige us equally, regardless of whether we are dealing with Catholics or with heretics. It is never allowed to lie, it is never allowed to violate someone else's right, it is never allowed to commit injustice, it is never allowed to be treacherous. If you admit only once that you can still do that licitly because it is to a heretic that you are lying, because it is a heretic's right that you are violating, and because it is a heretic who suffers from your perjury, will you then also say you are allowed to kill a heretic, steal his possessions, and prosecute him out of hatred? All these things are absurd and against divine law.

9. We can confirm this reasoning based on what I have said before in the following way: whatever is intrinsically and by its own nature evil and illicit can never take place in a good and licit way, no matter under which pretext. Lying, violating someone else's right, injustice, and perjury are intrinsically and by their own nature evil and illicit. Therefore, they can never take place in a good and licit way, no matter under which pretext. So whether you are lying, perfidious, unjust, and treacherous to Catholics or to heretics, you are equally guilty, and you commit an equal crime.

10. Second, it is confirmed by Scripture in the following way: when the faithful make agreements with pagans and worshipers of idols, they must keep their faith with them in all licit and honest matters; from this it follows they must also do this when they deal with heretics. The latter are, after all, not in a worse condition in this respect than the former. Quite the contrary: heretics have even closer ties with the faithful because they acknowledge one true God just as they do, whereas pagans who worship idols do not acknowledge him. The preceding argument is confirmed by the example of Joshua and other kings of the people of Israel, who concluded a peace agreement with the Gibeonites, infidels and worshipers of idols. Even though they were

deceived by Gibeonites, they still kept the faith they had given them, so faithfully and honestly they did not only spare their lives—this was the subject of the agreement—but even protected them in the war against their neighboring enemies.

11. That they were right in doing so and should be praised for it—yes, that they even had to do it—can be proved with three arguments. First, by the authority of Joshua himself and the other kings. For when many common people thought they could rightfully kill the Gibeonites and did not need to keep their faith with them since they had been deceived, their kings opposed them and said, "We have sworn to them by the Lord, the God of Israel, and now we may not touch them" (Josh. 9:19).

12. Second, the case was confirmed by a miracle. The Gibeonites were attacked by neighboring peoples because of the treaty they had signed with the Israelites. By authority of the treaty, they asked Joshua for protection. He did not hesitate. Joshua, heedful of their agreement and partnership, proceeded with his soldiers to stop the enemy and defend the Gibeonites. A battle started. To show that fidelity in agreements pleased him, God not only granted victory to the Israelites but also stood by them with a new miracle: he took hold of the sun and prevented it from setting so that they had even more time to kill the enemy. These are the words of the Scriptures: "The sun stopped in the midst of heaven and did not hurry to set for about a whole day. The Lord heeded the voice of man; the Lord fought for Israel" (Josh. 10:13).[10]

13. Third, just as God granted Joshua this victory because he kept his faith, he severely punished King Saul (and his entire people) for betraying his faith. This is what happened. The Gibeonites had concluded an agreement with Joshua to spare their life, as has been said before. More than a century later, King Saul killed many of them, notwithstanding the agreement. But his act did not go unpunished. As the Scriptures read, "Then there was a famine in the days of David for three years, year after year." So you see the punishment here. The reason is explained in the following:

---

[10] Ed. note: The quotation includes part of v. 14.

David consulted the Lord. And the Lord said, "It is because of Saul—there is bloodguilt on Saul and his house because he killed the Gibeonites."

So the king sent for the Gibeonites and spoke to them, "What shall I do for you? And how shall I make atonement, that you may bless the heritage of the Lord?"

The Gibeonites said to him, "It is not a matter of silver and gold, but against Saul and his house. Let seven of his sons be given to us, so that we may crucify them before the Lord in Gibeah."

And the king said, "I will give them." And he gave them into the hands of the Gibeonites, and they crucified them on the mountain before the Lord. And God showed mercy again after this had happened. (2 Sam. 21:1–14)[11]

You see how severely Saul and his descendants were punished because he had violated the faith he had given?

14. And there are similar examples. King Zedekiah violated his treaty with King Nebuchadnezzar of Babylon. He thought he could withdraw from it and act against his given faith, both because Nebuchadnezzar was a pagan and worshiper of idols and because he had been assaulting the Jewish people for many years already. What happened? Due to this treachery, he not only was punished with the loss of his kingdom and his eyes but also with the loathsome loss of his children and the destruction of his city.

15. Simeon and Levi, sons of Jacob, concluded an agreement with the Shechemites on mutual marriages, under one condition: all Shechemites had to be circumcised. This took place; they were all circumcised. But what did Simeon and Levi do? Against the agreement, they killed the circumcised. Under which pretext? That they wanted to take revenge for rape committed by the Shechemites. But because of their perfidy, their father rightly spoke to them: "Simeon and Levi are brothers, vessels of iniquity waging war. Let my soul not go into their council, and let my glory not be with them. For in their

---

[11] Ed. note: The quotation is fragmentary.

anger they killed men, and in their willfulness they undermined a wall. Cursed be their anger."[12]

16. These examples are taken from sacred history. Now listen to the following taken from profane history. When Vladislav, king of Poland and Hungary, returned to his fatherland from war after having enjoyed great victories against Murad, the sultan of the Turks, he signed a truce with the enemy and confirmed it with an oath.[13] Shortly after, when a couple of Christian rulers called on him to go to war again, he began to doubt what was best to do. On the one hand, the glory of his recent victory and the exhortation of so many people excited him; on the other hand, the armistice signed with the enemy drew him in another direction. In the end, the former part of him won, and so, against his given faith, he attacked Murad. Both sides fought heavily. During the battle, as Murad saw he was being forced back and restrained because he had lost many of his men, he yelled, with a loud cry, "Christ! If you are God, as your Christians claim, take revenge on the perfidy of your believers because they invade me by force of arms against the sworn agreement." And a miracle happened. The tide of the battle suddenly turned. While he was fighting in the midst of the Turkish lines, Vladislav was beaten off his horse and beheaded—a punishment for his treachery. Johann Georg Scheid recounts this story, along with many others.[14]

---

[12] Ed. note: Gen. 49:5–7.

[13] Ed. note: The reference is to King Vladislav III (1424–1444) of the Jagiellon dynasty. He became ruler of Poland when he was barely ten years old, and of Hungary and Croatia at the age of sixteen. On November 10, 1444, he was killed at the Battle of Varna, on the Black Sea coast, by the troops of the Ottoman sultan Mehmed II and his father, Murad II. Just months earlier, in the summer of 1444, Vladislav had sworn a ten-year truce with Murad, causing the latter to retreat from power immediately. Taking advantage of this sudden retreat, Pope Eugene IV absolved Vladislav from his oath to prepare a new crusade. See Colin Imber, *The Ottoman Empire, 1300–1650: The Structure of Power* (Houndmills, Basingstoke, UK: Palgrave Macmillan, 2009), 23–24.

[14] Ed. note: Little is known about Johann Georg Scheid (Georgius Scheidius), except that he is the presumed editor of the posthumous publi-

17. I draw the following conclusion: If we must keep our faith with pagans, worshipers of idols and Turks, then why not with heretics? It makes no difference that heretics do not keep their faith with God. This does not concern the matter of contracts between humans, with which we are dealing here, but has to be left to divine judgment. That is a topic outside the scope of my disputation.

---

cation in 1595 of the disputation *De bello cum juratissimis Christianae fidei hostibus Turcis gerendo* (On waging war with the Turks, sworn enemies of the Christian faith), authored by a certain John, Count of Tarnov, in Poland and addressed to Emperor Charles V.

8

DO WE HAVE TO KEEP OUR FAITH WITH HERETICS WHEN THEY HAVE BEEN EXCOMMUNICATED?

1. Thus far I have shown that heresy alone, when there is no other objection, does not free us from the obligation of keeping our faith with heretics. Now we must ask some more specific questions: (1) Do we have to keep our faith with them in the case of excommunication? (2) And in marriage contracts? (3) In wartime? (4) And regarding safe conduct? I shall deal with each of these questions in a separate chapter.

2. In this chapter the question is this: Do we have to keep our faith with heretics when they have been excommunicated? Because Catholics teach that excommunicated heretics are to be avoided and that we should not trade with them, many people think that Catholics also proclaim we should not keep our faith with them. But this is incorrect, as keeping faith is a different matter altogether, as will become clear shortly. Here is how things are:

3. Heretics are to be avoided for two reasons: (1) because of their heresy and (2) because of their excommunication. On the basis of their heresy, they are to be avoided according to divine law and natural law in these three cases: first, in the case of illicit fellowship in religious matters; second, when there is danger of subversion; third, for the fear of scandal. The first conclusion to be drawn from this is that it

is not allowed to gather with them to celebrate religious services in the Calvinist way, just as it is not allowed to worship idols together with pagans. This so-called fellowship in religious matters is forbidden because it goes against true faith. The second consequence is that unlearned and simple men who are naturally frail and unstable must not deal with heretics a lot because they are easily perverted and misguided. Third, even the learned and unwavering must not linger with heretics when it is probable that their conduct will cause scandal to others. On the other hand, we must conclude that—these three cases aside—it is allowed to converse with heretics according to both divine and natural law, as long as the conversation is honest to others.

4. On the basis of their excommunication, heretics must be avoided in these three cases according to human ecclesiastical law: (1) during participation in the sacraments, (2) during public votes and prayers, and (3) at dinners and intimate gatherings. This is what St. Thomas and other theologians write in their commentaries on Peter Lombard's *Sentences*;[1] it is also proved by several passages from canon law, under many different headings. From this we must conclude that because of their excommunication (1) it is not allowed to be baptized by a heretic (unless perhaps in a case of necessity) or to marry one; (2) it is not allowed to pray for them in public; and (3) it is not allowed to enter into civil contracts with them, have dinner with them, or speak with them, even if there is no danger or scandal involved.

5. These ecclesiastical law provisions on avoiding excommunicated heretics have been established for two good reasons. First, it benefits the wrongdoers, for when they see they are being shunned they become ashamed and come to their senses, just as in the word of the apostle: "And have nothing to do with him, that he may be ashamed" (2 Thess. 3:14). See also the decision of Pope Innocent IV about the medicinal character of the punishment of excommunication cited in the *Liber Sextus*.[2] Second, it benefits and safeguards others lest they get infected, as we can read in Paul's first epistle to the Corinthians: "Do you not know that a little leaven leavens the whole lump?" (5:6). At this point

---

[1] Thomas Aquinas, *On the Sentences* 4.18.

[2] Liber Sextus 5.11.1.

it becomes clear that not only heretics but also other people are bound by this law: the former, as a punishment for their crime, to keep them apart from the fellowship of believers; the latter, healthy as they are, to prevent them from getting infected by their company.

6. However, since the Council of Constance,[3] this law on avoiding excommunicates is not as strict as it used to be. For even though all excommunicated people, on the basis of their excommunication, have to stay away from the community of believers, believers, conversely, are not bound to avoid their company unless they have been excommunicated by name or unless they have notoriously beaten clergymen. Pope Martin V made this decision at the Council of Constance in favor of the believers in the Bull *Ad evitanda scandala*,[4] as is indicated by St. Antonine of Florence,[5] Domingo de Soto,[6] Cajetan,[7] Henríquez,[8] Suárez,[9] and many others.

---

[3] Ed. note: The Council of Constance (1414–1418) is famous for condemning Jan Hus, an early church reformer in the kingdom of Bohemia, as a heretic. Sebastián Provvidente, "Hus's Trial in Constance: Disputatio aut inquisitio," in *A Companion to Jan Hus*, ed. Ota Pavlíček and František Šmahel (Leiden: Brill, 2015), 254–88.

[4] Ed. note: Pope Martin V's bull is discussed in F. E. Hyland, *Excommunication: Its Nature, Historical Development and Effects* (Washington, DC: Catholic University of America Press, 1928), 35–47.

[5] Antonine of Florence, *Summa of Moral Theology* 3.25.2 and 3.

[6] Soto, *On the Sentences* 4.22.1.4.

[7] Cajetan, *Summa*, s.v. "excommunicatio."

[8] Henríquez, *On Marriage* 3.5. Ed. note: Enrique Henríquez (1546–1608), Jesuit theologian, dedicated an entire book of his work *On Moral Theology* to marriage law, which was simply referred to as *On Marriage*.

[9] Suárez, *On Censures* 9.2.5. Ed. note: Francisco Suárez (1548–1617) is perhaps the most famous Jesuit scholastic theologian. He made a fundamental contribution to the protection of heretics' and excommunicates' rights. See Wim Decock, "Trust Beyond Faith: Re-Thinking Contracts with Heretics and Excommunicates in Times of Religious War," *Rivista Internazionale di Diritto Comune* 27 (2016): 301–28.

7. From this it follows first that, at least as far as common ecclesiastical law is concerned, it is licit for Catholics all across the German empire and most of its neighboring territories to have contact with heretics because at this time no one is, as far as I know, excommunicated by name on the ground of heresy. Whether there are notorious murderers of clergymen, everyone can find out in his own hometown. I said "as far as ecclesiastical law is concerned" because, according to natural and divine law, we are obliged to avoid all heretics (not on the basis of their excommunication, but of their heresy itself) in the three cases I described above—namely, the celebration of religious services or if there is danger of subversion or of a scandal. I also added "as far as *common* ecclesiastical law is concerned" because in certain places, especially in Italy and Spain, it is not licit to be in contact with heretics under particular laws and prohibitions.

8. Second, it follows that on their part, excommunicated people—no matter whether they are Catholics or heretics—are not allowed to spontaneously join the company of each other. For the qualification of the original prohibition by ecclesiastical law has not been put in place to benefit the excommunicated, but for the sake of the other believers, as we may deduce from the canon law provision introduced by Pope Martin V quoted above. However, if believers invite or request them to speak, dine, or enter into a contract with them, they are allowed to do so, as long as the matter is licit, because otherwise the privilege of the believers would be useless; see Francisco Suárez[10] and other authors.

9. Against this background, we have to examine the question whether we have to keep our faith with heretics when they have been excommunicated. Or to put it differently: Is excommunication alone a sufficient ground not to keep our faith with them? The answer is easy. Because from what I have said before it is an established fact that if they have not been excommunicated by name or if they do not belong to those notorious murderers of clergymen, they do not have to be avoided on the basis of excommunication. Accordingly, we can conclude agreements and contracts with them no less than with others, and thus we need to keep our faith with those heretics.

---

[10] Suárez, *On Censures* 15.8.7.

10. As far as heretics who have been excommunicated by name are concerned, a distinction needs to be made. If you concluded a contract with them before they were excommunicated, and if this contract was valid at that time, it does not become invalid by the mere fact of the subsequent excommunication, and you will still be obliged to stick to the faith you promised in it. The reason is that excommunication, being a sanction imposed by human law, does not carry more force than has been granted to it by human power. And there is no human constitution or law that grants that sanction the power to deprive someone else of the right he has on the basis of a legitimate contract. It would have that power if it were to rescind that legitimate contract and make it invalid. From this I conclude that if the excommunicated heretic continues to have the right he received on entering into a contract with you, you will without any doubt remain obliged in conscience to perform what is legally due to him.

11. But if you entered into a contract with them by the time they already had been excommunicated by name, you committed a sin by entering into this contract because you acted against the plain prohibition of the church not to deal with excommunicated people. The contract, however, is still valid if it is not deficient on any other ground. Therefore, you will be bound to keep your faith. We can deduce this from canon *Foelicis*[11] and from specific examples. For a marriage with an excommunicated person is still valid according to canon *Significasti*.[12] Similarly, one's religious vow is still valid after excommunication, as is made clear by canon *Cum illorum* and Abbas Panormitanus's commentary on it.[13] A donation made by the excommunicated person still holds too, according to canon *Inter dilectos*.[14]

---

[11] Liber Sextus 5.9.5.

[12] Dec. Greg. 4.7.6.

[13] Dec. Greg. 5.39.32. Ed. note: Abbas Panormitanus (1386–1445), born as Niccolò de' Tedeschi, was one of the most influential canon lawyers of the late Middle Ages. His view that debtors did not need to pay back debts to excommunicated creditors was criticized by the early modern scholastics. See Decock, "Trust Beyond Faith," 307.

[14] Dec. Greg. 3.24.8.

Therefore, we have to think the same about all other types of contracts if there is no other obstacle.

12. But here we face two objections. The first is that it is not allowed to deal with someone who has been excommunicated by name; and thus we should not have to keep our faith with him, especially if we are not able to do so unless we have contact with him. The second is that heretics seem to be deprived of their property rights and their right to temporal possessions through their excommunication, as we can read in canon *Cum secundum leges*: "The possessions of heretics are automatically confiscated."[15] If this is the case, no matter what we promise to them or in what way we conclude a contract with them, they surely have no single right to petition or claim anything. Consequently, we are not obliged to perform our promise to them.

13. Regarding the first objection, most experts agree that if you legitimately entered into a contract with someone who has been excommunicated by name, you will still be bound to keep your faith with him, and you cannot retain what you contractually owe him. No law would permit this. The experts disagree, however, on whether you have to keep your faith and pay your debts while he is still excommunicated, or whether you should rather wait until the excommunication is lifted. Francisco Suárez discusses this question.[16] Yet this difference of opinion is not very important for our argument first, because it is sufficient for us to show that one must keep his faith with heretics, even to those who have been excommunicated by name, regardless of when or how that must happen; second, because in Germany and its neighboring provinces there hardly exist people who have been excommunicated by name. This renders the decision over the question rather useless to us.

14. The second objection is more serious. Here the question is being asked whether excommunication deprives heretics of every form of dominion and temporal rights. Above, I have just mentioned that they are not being deprived, which is a fact. The objection follows from the following provision in canon law: "The possessions of heretics are

---

[15] Liber Sextus 5.2.19.

[16] Suárez, *On Censures* 15.8.

automatically confiscated"—and yes, this is the case, but not on the ground of their excommunication. In order to understand this better, we must take notice that a variety of punishments has been put into place against heretics, some under canon law, others under civil law. The *first punishment* is excommunication, according to several canons in the title *De haereticis* in the *Liber Extra*.[17] The *second* is deprivation of their property rights and of the jurisdiction over their subordinates, according to canon *Nos sanctorum* and canon *Iuratos*,[18] in which Popes Gregory VII and Urban II release subordinates bound by an oath from the duty to serve their excommunicated masters and even forbid them to do so. The *third punishment* is the deprivation of their right to temporal goods. The treasury acquires the right to these possessions, as is explained by canon *Cum secundum leges*, where we read, "We declare the possessions of heretics to be automatically confiscated."[19]

15. These, however, are merely the ecclesiastical punishments. The imperial laws are by no means milder, as is apparent from the many provisions in the title *De haereticis* in Justinian's Code. *To begin with*, the Emperors Arcadius and Honorius have punished them with large fines, according to law *Cuncti haeretici*.[20] *Second*, heretics have been punished with the confiscation of their worldly possessions by these same emperors and also by Emperor Theodosius in law *Manichaeos*.[21] *Third*, exile has been added as a sanction by Emperors Theodosius and Valentinian in law *Ariani*.[22] And *finally*, capital punishment for heretics was introduced by law *Quicunque*,[23] which Valentinian and Marcian rewrote as follows: "Let those be sentenced to death, who

---

[17] Dec. Greg. 5.7.7 (*Cum Christus*); Dec. Greg. 5.7.8 (*Sicut ait*); Dec. Greg. 5.7.9 (*Ad abolendam*); Dec. Greg. 5.7.13 (*Excommunicamus*).

[18] Dec. Grat. C.15 q.6 c.4 and c.5.

[19] Liber Sextus 5.2.19

[20] Cod. 1.5.3*pr*.

[21] Cod. 1.5.4*pr*.

[22] Cod. 1.5.5*pr*.

[23] Cod. 1.5.8*pr*.

attempted to spread unlawful teachings."[24] Regarding this matter, see St. Augustine,[25] who demonstrates that the magistrate has the authority to take up the sword against heretics, following Paul's epistle to the Romans: "For he does not bear the sword in vain. For he is the servant of God, an avenger who carries out God's wrath on the wrongdoer" (13:4).

16. Hence it easily becomes clear that it is not on the basis of their excommunication that heretics are deprived of their property rights and jurisdiction over their subordinates and over their worldly possessions. This deprivation is a punishment separate from the excommunication itself, imposed by a separate law. However, the difficulty remains: Can we, by force of this punishment, let go of the faith we promised to a heretic? We could be forced to deduce this from the objection just made. For if a heretic lacks any right and dominion over his worldly possessions, no matter on which ground, he will not have the right to demand anything from you either, and therefore, should he make a claim on the basis of the promise or agreement, you will not be bound to give it to him. *My answer to this*: Here I need to make two points that will clarify the case entirely. The first point: the canon laws and civil laws that established these punishments for heretics are merely penal laws. The second point is that laws of this kind do not entail the obligation to execute the punishment before a judge has rendered the verdict, as St. Thomas says.[26]

17. Three corollaries follow from this. *First*, even though by these penal laws heretics are deprived of the right to their temporal possessions, they still are not required to deprive themselves of them or hand them over to the treasury before the verdict of a judge. Thus

---

[24] Cod. 1.5.8.11 (*Eos vero*). Ed. note: Becanus's interpretation of this law can be criticized, as the words *ultimo supplicio* in the Latin text can also simply refer to the sanction mentioned in the previous sentence of law *Eos vero*, which is just a pecuniary fine.

[25] Augustine, *Letter (no. 93) to Vincent*; *Letter (no. 185) to Boniface*; *Answer to Petilian the Donatist* 2.84.184.

[26] Thomas Aquinas, *Summa theologiae* II.2, Q. 62, A. 3, ad 3.

write Sylvester,[27] Domingo de Soto,[28] Dr. Navarrus,[29] Gregory of Valencia,[30] Juan Azor,[31] and others. *Second*, even after the verdict of a judge they are not bound to hand over their own goods or offer them to the treasury because the execution of the punishment is not up to them, but to the officials of the judge or the treasury. However, they are obliged not to resist by force or by fraud. This we can find in Azor.[32] *Third*, as long as the heretic has not effectively been deprived of his goods according to the procedure of execution mentioned before, he still has the right of use and usufruct over them. He even enjoys the right to donate them or appoint an heir, as long as there is no fraud or deceit involved. This is the view of Sylvester and other authors and can be found in canon *Cum secundum leges*. The reason for this is based on the will of the legislator and on established custom.

18. So from this you can easily conclude when you owe something to a heretic on the basis of the faith of a promise or an agreement, whether you are obliged to fulfill it or not. Before the verdict of a judge and the execution of punishment, you must perform the promise to him; after the verdict, you must perform to the judge or to the treasury when asked. Yet this happens very rarely, especially in Germany and its neighboring provinces. It is, after all, unusual for the treasury to seize the goods of a heretic, unless something else intervenes.

---

[27] Sylvester, *Summa silvestrina*, s.v. "haeresis 1," no. 12.

[28] Soto, *On Justice and Right* 1.6.6.

[29] Dr. Navarrus, *Enchiridion or Manual for Confessors and Penitents* 23.66.

[30] Valencia, *Theological Commentaries* 3.5.11.3. Ed. note: Gregorio de Valencia (1549–1603), Jesuit theologian at the University of Ingolstadt, played a major role in handing down the teachings of the School of Salamanca to Germany.

[31] Azor, *Moral Institutes* 8.12.3. Ed. note: Juan Azor (1536–1603) taught at the Jesuit colleges in Alcalá and Rome. His *Moral Institutes*, or *Institutiones morales*, became a reference work on moral theology.

[32] Azor, *Moral Institutes* 8.12.4.

9

DO WE HAVE TO KEEP OUR FAITH WITH HERETICS IN MARRIAGE CONTRACTS?

1. Marriage has two sides to it. It is a civil contract and a sacrament. Of course the particular difficulty here arises because of its sacramental aspect. The Catholic teaching is twofold. First, even though one should not easily enter into marriage contracts with heretics, once they have been concluded, they are valid. Second, in these marriages one must keep marital fidelity. I will have to explain both points.

2. *The first conclusion.* If Catholics enter into a marriage with heretics and there is no other objection than heresy, the contract is valid. We can find this in St. Thomas,[1] Dr. Navarrus,[2] Gregory of Valencia,[3] and others at different places. The reason for this is that heresy is not counted among the diriment impediments—namely, the impediments that affect the validity of the marriage. Hence, it does not prevent the marriage from being valid, at least if the marriage does not suffer from another defect. Even though disparity of cult counts among the diri-

---

[1] Thomas Aquinas, *On the Sentences* 4.39.1.1.5.

[2] Dr. Navarrus, *Enchiridion or Manual for Confessors and Penitents* 22.49.

[3] Valencia, *Theological Commentaries* 3.10.5.3.

ment impediments, it concerns the difference between a believer and a nonbeliever who has not been baptized, *not* the difference between a Catholic and a baptized heretic. This is the common opinion of the experts and established practice. The reason for this distinction is that the right to receive all other sacraments is granted through baptism, which is like a door to the remaining sacraments. So those who received baptism have this right; others do not have it. Now marriage between Christians is a sacrament under the new law.

3. We can find an objection to this in canon 72 of the Sixth Synod: "An orthodox man is not allowed to unite with a heretic woman, neither is an orthodox woman allowed to unite with a heretic man. However, should something of this sort occur, we must consider this marriage invalid, and the nefarious union must be dissolved."[4] So here we have a clear decision about the nullity of a marriage contracted with a heretic. *My answer to this*: The canons of this particular council do not bear any authority, as Robert Bellarmine[5] and many other authors have shown. Hence Bede the Venerable calls these canons the product of "an erroneous synod" and says that Pope Sergius disapproved of them.[6]

---

[4] Ed. note: The reference is to the Council in Trullo, convened by Emperor Justinian II in 691. It is considered a general council by the Orthodox Church. In the early modern period, canon 72 of the *Concilium Trullanum* was no longer followed by the majority of the churches following the Byzantine rite. See Udo Breitbach, *Die Vollmacht der Kirche Jesu Christi über die Ehen der Getauften. Zur Gesetzesunterworfenheit der Ehen nichtkatholischer Christen* (Rome: Pontifical Gregorian University, 1998), 112n2.

[5] Bellarmine, *On the Roman Pontiff* 2.28; *On Councils* 1.7. Ed. note: Robert Bellarmine (1542–1621) was a major Jesuit theologian who taught at the Jesuit Colleges in Louvain and Rome. His theories about the indirect secular power of the church and the relationship between the Catholic Church and other Christian sects had a lasting impact on the church's ecclesiology. Becanus defended Bellarmine's view of state-church relationships during the English debate over the oath of allegiance. See Stefania Tutino, *Empire of Souls: Robert Bellarmine and the Christian Commonwealth* (Oxford: Oxford University Press, 2010), 211–60.

[6] Bede, *A Chronicle of the Six Ages of the World*, in the time of Justinian. Ed. note: PL 90, col. 568.

4. *The second conclusion.* Under such a contract, it being valid and legitimate, the spouses must certainly remain faithful to one another in all those matters that pertain to the honest enjoyment of marriage. This is already the case with any other legitimate and valid contract; it is much more so in marriage, which is indissoluble altogether. Hence we read in the gospel of Matthew: "Therefore a man shall leave his father and mother and hold fast to his wife, and the two shall become one flesh" (19:5). And a little later: "What therefore God has joined together, let no man separate."[7] And in Luke: "Everyone who divorces his wife and marries another commits adultery, and he who marries a woman divorced from her husband commits adultery" (16:18). And in the first letter to the Corinthians: "To the married I give this charge (not I, but the Lord): the wife should not separate from her husband (but if she does, she should remain unmarried or else be reconciled to her husband), and the husband should not divorce his wife" (7:10).

5. These are all general rules on marital fidelity. Theologians provide us with the particularities and teach us we must especially look at these three rules regarding marital fidelity. The *first rule* is that no one can have a relationship with a third person as long as the other spouse is still alive. For the chain of marriage is indissoluble and cannot be broken in a different way other than through the death of one of the spouses. The testimonies quoted above pertain to this rule, as well as this verse from the letter to the Romans: "For a married woman is bound by law to her husband while he lives, but if her husband dies, she is released from the law of her husband. Accordingly, she will be called an adulteress if she lives with another man while her husband is alive" (7:2). The *second rule* is that spouses should render the debt that they owe to each other, as is evident from the first epistle to the Corinthians: "The husband should render the debt to his wife, and likewise the wife to her husband. For the wife does not have power over her own body, but the husband does. Likewise the husband does not have power over his own body, but the wife does. Do not deprive one another from this debt, except perhaps by consent for a limited

---

[7] Ed. note: Matt. 19:6.

time, that you may devote yourselves to prayer" (7:3).[8] The *third rule* is that spouses should live together and run a family together, but in such a way that the wife is subjected to her husband. For the apostle warns in his first letter to the Corinthians that "the husband is the head of the wife" (11:3). And in the first letter to Timothy he says, "I do not permit a woman to teach or to exercise authority over a man" (2:12).

6. So marital fidelity consists of these three things. And regarding the first rule, faith must be kept in such a way that a Catholic man will never be allowed to marry another woman while his wife is still alive, even if she is a heretic. The passages quoted from the Scriptures make this crystal clear. However, with regard to the bed and cohabitation, a separation may sometimes be possible for legitimate reasons, even if in such cases the bond of marriage remains valid. This has been established by the Council of Trent.[9] Theologians list three grounds for such a separation. The *first* is when both spouses agree and devote themselves to perpetual continence and enter into the religious life: "And everyone who has left his house or wife for my name's sake will receive a hundredfold and will inherit eternal life" (Matt. 19:29). The *second* ground for a separation can be a crime committed by one of the spouses, such as adultery. About this, see Matthew 5:32: "Everyone who sends away his wife, except on the ground of sexual immorality, makes her commit adultery." The crime could also be grave violence, imperiling the other spouse's life, or incitements to sin: "And if your hand or your foot causes you to sin, cut it off and throw it away" (Matt. 18:8), or something similar. The *third* reason could be leprosy or some other horrible and contagious disease. See Bellarmine,[10] Valencia,[11] and others.

7. Thus from all this I conclude that if a Catholic man accepts a heretic woman as his wife and she allows him to live, educate their children, and manage their family affairs according to Catholic rites,

---

[8] Ed. note: The quotation continues into v. 5.

[9] Council of Trent, session 24, decree 8.

[10] Bellarmine, *On Marriage* 14.

[11] Valencia, *Theological Commentaries* 3.4.2.

and there is no other disgraceful act or disease impeding their conjugal life, he must keep his faith with her in all circumstances no less than if she were a Catholic. But if, on the other hand, she were to commit adultery, tries to persuade him to believe her heresy, or raises their children in heresy, he may send her away while the conjugal bond remains in place nonetheless. But what if the man promised from the beginning to satisfy himself with his heretic wife educating the children? That is a filthy promise, invalid by itself; he is not bound to keep it.

10

Do We Have to Keep Our Faith with Heretics When It Comes to Freedom of Religion?

1. Freedom of religion can be brought about in two different ways: first, when in a certain kingdom, province, or city each person is granted the freedom to think and follow whatever he wants, in such a way that he is free to be either a Catholic, Lutheran, Calvinist, or Anabaptist; second, when only heretics are given the freedom to practice their religion among Catholics. The question here is this: If a Catholic prince or magistrate makes an agreement with heretics on either of these possibilities, should he subsequently keep his faith?

2. On this matter the decision must be made as follows: (1) Freedom of religion is by all means forbidden and goes against divine precept. (2) Freedom of religion is destructive to the state. (3) It must not be ordered, authorized, or introduced by any prince or magistrate, but rather be impeded and overthrown by all means that are appropriate and possible, at least if that can be done conveniently. (4) However, if this cannot be done conveniently, causing great damage or evil to the state, it can be tolerated for a while. (5) If it is being tolerated in this manner and an agreement has been made, faith must be kept. This is the Catholic view, which I will explain in four conclusions.

3. *The first conclusion.* Freedom of faith or religion is plainly forbidden and against Christian doctrine. This becomes clear throughout the entire New Testament. Yes, there are many places in the Gospels from which we know for certain that Christ demanded one single faith and forbade various and multiple forms of faith. *To start with*: he wanted there to be only one church, one flock, one shepherd, and one baptism. But these cannot exist without the unity of faith. *Second*, he wanted his disciples to keep away from false prophets, but with multiple religions, it is inevitable that there are some true and some false prophets. Therefore, if they need to be excluded, we should retain one faith only and drive out the rest. *Third*, he wanted his church to be everlasting, impossible for any force of death to resist. But it cannot be everlasting if there is not one faith for all, as Luke himself testifies: "Every kingdom divided against itself collapses."[1]

4. The apostle affirms this in well-spoken words: "I appeal to you, brothers, to watch out for those who cause divisions and create obstacles contrary to the doctrine that you have been taught; avoid them" (Rom. 16:17); "But even if we or an angel from heaven should preach to you a gospel contrary to the one we preached to you, let him be accursed" (Gal. 1:8); "I appeal to you, brothers, by the name of our Lord Jesus Christ, that all of you agree and that there be no divisions among you" (1 Cor. 1:10); "For God is not a God of confusion, but of peace" (1 Cor. 14:33); "one Lord, one faith, one baptism" (Eph. 4:5); "Do not be led away by diverse and strange teachings" (Heb. 13:9). You see how seriously, how eagerly, and how intensely the apostle urges us to keep unity of faith. But that would not be possible if we were to give way to religious freedom.

5. *The second conclusion.* The freedom that we are speaking about is damaging and dangerous to the state, not just with respect to the salvation of the souls (there can be no doubt about this) but also with respect to peace and political tranquility, which cannot be kept without unity of faith. Christ himself testifies to this when he says, "Every kingdom divided against itself collapses."[2] All sacred and profane

---

[1] Ed. note: Luke 11:17.

[2] Ed. note: Luke 11:17.

authors testify to this, both Christians and pagans. Justus Lipsius, among others, deals with this argument in a brilliant way in his *Book on the Unity of Religion against a Disputant*.[3]

6. And there is an almost infinite number of examples at hand. How many masses did the Arians stir up in the entire East? How many the Macedonians in Greece? And the Donatists and Circumcellions in Africa? St. Augustine writes about this in his letter to Januarius the Donatist:

> Your followers are doing terrible things to us. They do not just beat us up with sticks and cut us with knives but they also throw lime mixed up with vinegar at us to blind our eyes—an incredible crime they came up with. Just to plunder our houses they made enormous and horrible armaments, and as soon as they are armed with them, they run around in different directions, threatening and committing murder, robbery, fire, and blindness. Because of these acts I feel forced to write to you and utter my complaints.[4]

And a little later:

> You say you suffer from persecution, and yet your armed men kill us with branches and knives. You say you suffer from persecution, and yet your armed men burn down our houses with lime and vinegar.

In this letter he gives many more examples along the same line. These are similar to the things the Iconoclasts and the Albigenses did in the Roman Empire, the Hussites in Bohemia, and the Calvinists in

---

[3] Ed. note: The disputant referred to is Dirck Coornhert (1522–1599), a staunch defender of religious liberty who had attacked the less liberal views expressed by Lipsius in his *Politics*. See Gerrit Voogt, "Primacy of Individual Conscience or Primacy of the State? The Clash between Dirck Volckertsz. Coornhert and Justus Lipsius," *Sixteenth Century Journal* 28, no. 4 (1997): 1231–49.

[4] Augustine, *Letter (no. 88) to Januarius* 8.

England, Belgium, France, and Poland. It wearies me to mention all of them; they are too well known, too monstrous.

7. And why would this spark any wonder? There has never been a family made up of different religions where peace has not been disturbed. Take, for example, the quarrel between Isaac and Ishmael in Abraham's family; between Jacob and his father-in-law, Laban, in Mesopotamia; between Moses and his wife, Zipporah, when they were heading to Egypt. So how could one hope for peace and harmony in an entire kingdom, province, or city when there is the greatest dissension on religion and faith? Julian the Apostate already realized this: when he wished to disturb and overthrow the Christian church, he introduced liberty and a variety of doctrines. Ammianus writes about this—he is the source on which Lipsius draws at the place cited above.

8. There are two reasons for this. First, where there is discord of spirit, there cannot be peace; and there is the greatest discord of spirit possible where there are sects, schisms, and a variety of doctrines. Therefore, there can be no place for peace and concord. Second, it is impossible to preserve unity and friendship among the arrogant, and wherever there is heresy, there is arrogance; hence, we think in vain about maintaining unity. From this I infer the following. Heretics are arrogant, definitely if they disagree with us on the administration of sacraments, if they ruin our churches and monasteries, destroy altars and religious images, mock the bishops and the clergy, if they despise of our rites and ceremonies and execrate the Eucharist, fasting, and holidays. How could they then be able to keep peace and harmony with us in political matters? That is not in line with their habits and character. Who have ever been more unanimous than the people of Judah and the people of Israel? But later they erected altar against altar, temple against temple, and soon they were dispersed and disunited in an inexplicable discord.

9. *The third conclusion.* Freedom of religion must not be ordained, authorized, or introduced by any Catholic ruler or magistrate, but rather be impeded and overthrown by all means, at least if that can be done conveniently, first, because it goes against divine precept; second, because it disturbs peace and tranquillity in the state. Both points have been made clear above. This is why the church has convened councils

on so many occasions—namely, in order to preserve the unity of faith and prevent liberty and variety of religion from arising. And this is where the most severe laws of the best emperors come from:

> There must be no single place for the ceremonies of heretics and no occasion for the clement display of their stubborn minds. May all know that even if that kind of people obtained some special imperial rescript by fraud, it is not valid. May that mob of heretics be denied access to their illicit congregations; may the name of the one and greatest God be celebrated everywhere. Our standard must always be obedience to the Nicaean faith; it was transmitted, of old, by our ancestors and confirmed by the testimony and practice of the divine religion.[5]

And further on: "If seditious outbreak is attempted, we order to end the fury and expel the heretics from their own city walls; all Catholic churches throughout the world must be brought back under the power of the orthodox bishops who hold on to the Nicaean faith."[6] And then there is law *Cuncti haeretici*: "All heretics must know with absolute certainty that they shall be deprived of all their places."[7] See multiple laws at the same place.

10. And the emperors did not act differently. Constantine the Great condemned Arius and sent him into exile together with Eusebius and Theognides, and he threatened to exile all who would not comply with the Council of Nicaea. The military demanded Jovian to become emperor. He confirmed he would take up supreme command only after all soldiers serving him and the Roman Empire testified that they wanted to profess the one Christian faith, obviously because he realized that with a variety of religions, the power of the emperor could not be firm enough. Let us not even talk about Theodosius the Great and Theodosius II, Marcian, Justinian, Aurelian, Gratian, Justin,

---

[5] Cod. 1.1.2*pr*.
[6] Cod. 1.1.2.2.
[7] Cod. 1.5.3*pr*.

Charlemagne, and others like them; their histories are well known. Whoever wishes may consult Baronio and others.[8]

11. Now I come to the bishops. The first who comes to mind is St. Ambrose, a most fierce advocate and promoter of the unity of faith. Emperor Valentinian, persuaded by his mother, Justina, an Arian woman, ordered him to allow the Arians a sanctuary, asserting there would be peace and tranquility in the Empire from the moment those belonging to a different religion would be granted a fixed place to worship.

And what did Ambrose do then? Listen to what he himself wrote about it in the letter to his sister Marcellina:

> The day after I received the letter in which you told me how you had been troubled in your dreams, a heavy weight of troubles began to assail me. It was not now the Portian Basilica—that is, the one outside the walls—which was demanded, but the new basilica—that is, the one within the walls—which is bigger. In the first place some chief men, counselors of state, appealed to me to give up the basilica and restrain the people from raising any commotion. I replied, respecting good order, that a bishop could not give up God's house.[9]

And further on:

> I was convened by the attendants and tribunes to give up the basilica without delay. They maintained that the emperor was exercising his right since he had supreme power over all

---

[8] Ed. note: Cesare Baronio (1538–1607), a doctor in civil and canon law, went on to become a priest in the Congregation of the Oratory. At the request of Philip Neri, the founder of his order, Baronio wrote the *Ecclesiastical Annals*, a Catholic history of the church in twelve volumes published between 1588 and 1607. He was appointed cardinal and librarian of the Vatican Library by Pope Clement VIII.

[9] Ed. note: Ambrose, *Letter (no. 20) to Marcellina* 1–2. The translation is borrowed, with adaptations, from the anonymous 1881 English edition of Ambrose's letters at http://www.tertullian.org/fathers/ambrose_letters_02_letters11_20.htm#Letter20.

things. I replied that if he required of me what was my own, like my estate and my money, I would not refuse it, but that sacred things were not subject to the power of the emperor.[10]

He goes on:

> Eventually they order me to deliver up the basilica. I reply, "It is not lawful for me to deliver it up, nor for you, the emperor, to receive it. By no law can you violate the house of a private man, so do you think that the house of God may be taken away?" They assert the emperor can do anything he wants, that all things are his. I reply, "But do not burden your conscience with the thought that you have any right as emperor over sacred things. Exalt not yourself. If you want to reign longer, be subject to God. It is written, 'God's to God and Caesar's to Caesar.' The palace belongs to the emperor, the churches to the bishop. To you is committed jurisdiction over public, not over sacred buildings." Again the emperor is said to have issued his order, claiming that he ought to have one basilica. I answered, "It is not licit for you to have her. What do you want to do with an adulteress? For a church that is not bound with Christ in lawful wedlock is an adulteress."[11]

And at the end of the letter he writes:

> Last, Calligonus the Grand Chamberlain ventured to address himself specially to me. "As long as I live, I will have your head if you continue to despise Valentinian. I will have your head." I replied, "May God grant you to fulfill your threat: I shall suffer as becomes a bishop; you will act as befits an eunuch."[12]

This is enough from Ambrose's letter.

---

[10] Ed. note: Ambrose, *Letter (no. 20) to Marcellina* 8.

[11] Ed. note: Ambrose, *Letter (no. 20) to Marcellina* 19.

[12] Ed. note: Ambrose, *Letter (no. 20) to Marcellina* 28.

12. John Chrysostom was of similar disposition when he addressed Commander Gainas, an Arian man. Theodoret describes what happened:

> A certain Gainas, a Scythian, barbarous in character and of brutal, tyrannical disposition, was at that time a military commander. He was feared not only by all the rest but also by the emperor himself. He was imbued with the Arian pest and requested the emperor to grant him one of the churches. Arcadius replied that he would see to it and at the same time promised to have it done. He then sent for the divine John, told him of Gainas's request, reminded him of his power, and hinted at his tyrannical project. He begged John to bridle Gaias's anger by donating the temple. "But," said that noble man to him, "do not order me to make such a promise nor to give what is sacred to the dogs. I will never tolerate that the worshipers and praisers of the divine Word are expelled, and that their church is given to people who commit blasphemy against the Lord. Have no fear, emperor, of that barbarian. Call us both, me and him, before you, and listen in silence to what we say each. I am sure that I will both curb the tongue of that man and persuade him not to demand what it is wrong to grant him." The emperor was delighted with that proposition and on the next day summoned both men before him. Gainas requested the execution of the promise, but the great John said in reply that it was not licit for an emperor who intended to observe the principles of piety to make plans against the sacred things. Gainas nevertheless insisted that a temple should be given to him. To which the great John replied, "The holy temple is open to you. Nobody prevents you from praying there when you want."
>
> "But I," said Gainas, "belong to another sect, and I demand to have a holy temple with them. My request is not unreasonable since I have fought so many battles for the Roman people."
>
> "But," said John, "you have been granted greater rewards for your labors since you are a military commander now and gifted with consular honor. Just consider what you were before and

what you have become now; consider your indigence in the past and your present prosperity. Look at the clothes you were wearing before crossing the Ister and what you are wearing now. Just realize how small your labors were in comparison with the greatness of your rewards. Do not be ungrateful to those who have shown you that honor." With these words the famous teacher of the entire world silenced Gainas and compelled him to stand dumb. After a certain time, however, the tyranny that he had long contrived was revealed in the open. He gathered his troops in Thrace and went out ravaging and plundering fields and towns. When the news of this reached them, both magistrates and subjects started to panic. No one was found willing to march against him. No one thought it safe to approach him with a diplomatic mission. Everyone dreaded his cruel and barbarous character. Then, when everyone else had retreated in fear, this great chief was persuaded to leave on a diplomatic mission. He took no heed of the dispute that has been related or of the conflict it had brought about and readily set out for Thrace with a delegation. No sooner did Gainas hear of the arrival of the envoy than he remembered the liberty with which he had defended the principles of piety. He made a long trip to meet John, placed his right hand on his eyes, and even brought his children to his saintly knees. This is how virtue excels and makes blush even the strongest.[13]

These are the words of Theodoret, bishop of Cyrus, on the perseverance of Chrysostom in fighting for the unity of faith and religion.

13. And what shall I say about Pope Leo the Great, who rebuked Anatolius, the bishop of Constantinople, because he allowed people professing another religion than the one Catholic faith to live together with Catholics?[14] Or about St. Augustine, who encouraged his friend Olympius to proclaim the laws of the emperor against Donatist heretics, for no other reason than his view that it is neither possible nor

---

[13] Theodoret of Cyrus, *Ecclesiastical History* 5.33.

[14] Leo the Great, *Letter (no. 85) to Anatolius.*

desirable to join various sects together with the one Catholic faith?[15] It would be too elaborate to mention all other authors who strictly outlawed doctrinal dissensions from the church of Christ.

14. *The fourth conclusion.* A Catholic prince or magistrate must impede religious freedom by all means, as I said before. If, however, he cannot do this without causing too much harm to the public good, he may tolerate it as a lesser evil to avoid a greater, which would have followed otherwise. This conclusion is founded on the well-known axiom "Choose the lesser of two evils," at least if we are not capable of avoiding both. And the reason for this is that in such a case the lesser evil is not chosen because it is evil, but as a useful means to avoid a greater evil, and consequently the evil is chosen because it is a useful good. This is the view of the most venerable authors. See, for example, St. Thomas.[16] On the basis of this principle, he proves that the rites of pagans and heretics may be tolerated to prevent a greater evil. See also Cajetan at the same place,[17] Gregory of Valencia,[18] Molina,[19] and many others. St. Augustine was of the same opinion when he wrote, "Remove prostitutes from this world, and you will throw everything into confusion through lust."[20] Gregory the Great wrote a lot along the same line.[21]

15. We can draw the same conclusion from Christ's parable of the weeds in Matthew 13. When the servants asked their master of the house, "Then do you want us to go and gather the weeds?" he replied, "No, lest in gathering the weeds you root up the wheat along with them. Let both grow together until the harvest."[22] Christ wanted to say that sometimes one ought to tolerate heretics in the midst of Catholics,

---

[15] Augustine, *Letter (no. 97) to Olympius.*

[16] Thomas Aquinas, *Summa theologiae* II.2, Q. 10, A. 11.

[17] Cajetan, *Commentaries on the Secunda Secundae* Q. 10, A. 11.

[18] Valencia, *Theological Commentaries* 3.1.10.7.

[19] Molina, *On Justice and Right* 2.335.

[20] Augustine, *On Order* 2.4.

[21] Cited in Dec. Grat. Dist.13 c.2.

[22] Ed. note: vv. 28–29.

especially when there is danger to eradicate the Catholics too if you root out the heretics. Maldonado nicely deals with this issue in his commentary on this parable.[23]

16. *The fifth conclusion.* If a Catholic prince or magistrate comes to an agreement with heretics about tolerating freedom of religion and this cannot be prevented without doing greater damage, he must keep his faith without any doubt, as has been proved from what has been said above. For faith needs to be kept in all licit and honorable pacts, and tolerating freedom of religion to avoid a greater evil is licit and honorable. A Catholic prince may lawfully and honorably conclude an agreement about tolerating it. So in that case he must keep his faith.

---

[23] Ed. note: The Jesuit theologian Juan Maldonado (1534–1583) published an influential commentary on the Gospels. Luke Murray, "A History of Historiography on Jesuit Exegesis," *Jesuit Historiography Online*, ed. Robert A. Maryks (Leiden: Brill, 2016), http://dx.doi.org/10.1163/2468-7723_jho_COM_193804.

11

DO WE HAVE TO KEEP OUR FAITH WITH HERETICS IN WARTIME?

1. A Catholic ruler may wage war against heretics for two reasons: first, for religious reasons; second, for a civil cause. When a war breaks out for religious reasons, I have already explained to what extent one may make agreements about freedom of religion. If it is for a civil cause, we can look at various aspects of the heretics against whom we wage war: (1) the fact that they are heretics, (2) the fact that they have been excommunicated, (3) the fact that they are enemies, and (4) the fact that they favor an unjust cause. As far as their heresy and excommunication is concerned: from what has been stated before, it is already clear what needs to be done. These two grounds do not mean that we do not need to keep our faith with them. Questions still arise over the two other aspects.

2. *The first conclusion.* If you consider nothing but the fact that they are your enemies, you have to keep your faith with heretics with whom you are at war. You have to do so in every way, in all promises and agreements that would be licit and honorable in other circumstances as well. This is the teaching of St. Thomas.[1] It can also be deduced

---

[1] Thomas Aquinas, *Summa theologiae* II.2, Q. 40, A. 3.

from St. Augustine. He literally said, "When faith has been given it needs to be kept, even to an enemy against whom we wage war."[2] And in Ambrose we read, "We may understand how great justice is when we see that she is not bound by places, persons, or times; she even extends to our enemies in such a way that if you agreed with an enemy on a place or day to fight, it should be considered unjust if you prevent it from happening at that place and time."[3] And shortly afterward, he writes, "Thus it is clear we must observe the virtues of faith and justice even in wartime, and there can be no decency whatsoever if faith is violated."

3. The reason for this is that we are obliged to keep our faith on the basis of the virtues of truth, fidelity, justice, and religion. This obligation following from these virtues does not disappear when the promisee is an enemy or rival. Quite the contrary; Christ explicitly orders us not just to love our friends but also our enemies: "But I say to you, love your enemies, so that you may be sons of your Father who is in heaven; he makes the sun rise on the evil and on the good" (Matt. 5:44).[4] We are bound to observe charity toward our enemies and foes. Why, then, would we not be bound in a similar way by the virtues of truth, fidelity, justice, and religion? And if it is sinful to hate your enemy, why would it not also be sinful to violate your faith with him?

4. There is, however, one general exception to this rule. We are not obliged to keep our faith with an enemy when he himself does not keep his faith with us, according to this rule of law in the *Liber Sextus*: "He will demand another to keep faith with him in vain, who refuses to keep the faith that has been given to him."[5] The proverb also refers to this: "With the breaker of faith, faith may be broken."[6] Therefore, if a ceasefire has been agreed on for a certain amount of time and the enemy does not observe it, we are not obliged to keep our promise

---

[2] Cited in Dec. Grat. C.23 q.1 c.3.

[3] Ambrose, *On Duties* 1.29.

[4] Ed. note: The quotation includes part of v. 45.

[5] Liber Sextus 5, *De regulis iuris* 75.

[6] *Frangenti fidem fides frangatur eidem*. Ed. note: See 7.2 above (p. 52n2).

to him either, even if it had been affirmed under oath. For an agreement always includes the following implied condition: provided you also respect the agreement; provided you keep your promise as well.

5. *The second conclusion.* If you merely consider that they are promoting an unjust cause, you have to treat heretics with whom you are at war in the same way you treat Catholics favoring an unjust cause. In this case, their condition is the same. Therefore, one must obey the following general rules. The *first* is, even though your enemy, whoever it is, favors an unjust cause, if you still freely made an agreement with him that would otherwise be licit and honorable in such a way that there is no force, fear, or deceit from his side involved, you will be bound to keep your faith with him. The *second* is, if he made you to agree by force, fear, or deceit, you may rescind the agreement following what has been written above.[7]

6. One may object by quoting the example of Joshua. Even though he had been misled into concluding an agreement with the Gibeonites, he remained nevertheless convinced that he had to keep his faith and must not rescind the agreement. My answer to this is that Joshua wanted to keep his faith, not exactly by virtue of the agreement but because of the oath he had taken and with which he had sealed the agreement. We can read this in Joshua: "We have sworn to them in the name of the Lord, the God of Israel, and therefore we may not touch them" (9:19).

---

[7] 3.4ff.

12

DO WE HAVE TO KEEP OUR FAITH WITH HERETICS REGARDING SAFE CONDUCT?

1. By safe conduct we mean the public faith and security to go to a certain place and to return again, as is apparent from Bartolus's commentaries on law *Utimur*, law *Relegati*, and law *Proximum*.[1]

2. Safe conduct can be guaranteed in two different ways: first, by general law,[2] as is the case when a person is granted security against violence unjustly threatening him, even if justice should not be violated; second, by particular law,[3] partially derogating from the general law, as is the case when someone is granted security against any kind of violence, whether the violence is wielded justly or unjustly against that person, especially in the case concerned.

3. The first type of safe conduct—granted by general law—has been described by Mynsinger: "When someone has been granted security or safe conduct, we must understand this solely as protection against violence that is factually committed against the law. I remember a case

---

[1] Dig. 47.12.5; Dig. 48.19.4; Dig. 48.4.1*pr*. Bartolus, *Commentary on the Digestum novum*.

[2] *ius commune*.

[3] *ius speciale*.

where someone had been caught for some wrongdoing or crime. He enjoyed safe conduct. But when he requested 'a court order to release him'[4] and 'a summons to have him see,'[5] the judges did not grant him those procedural remedies."[6] Eberhard Speckhan, professor of law in Helmstedt, speaks about safe conduct in the same manner, quoting several authors expressing the same view.[7] There is also a legal formula that the Saxons use on the basis of the Constitutio Criminalis Carolina: "We, the public authorities, give you our word[8] that you will be able to defend your case in court, that you will be protected against violence, but not that you will be protected against the execution of the law."[9]

---

[4] *mandatum de relaxando.*

[5] *citatio ad videndum.*

[6] Mynsinger, *Observations on the Imperial Chamber Court* 1.82. Ed. note: Joachim Mynsinger von Frundeck (1514–1588), a German jurist who became the vice president of the Lutheran University of Helmstedt, is famous for his collection of observations on the deliberations behind the decisions of the Imperial Chamber Court, where he served as a judge from 1548 to 1556. Andreas Gail (1526–1587) imitated this groundbreaking project. Their works were often published together. Peter Oestmann, "Observationes," in *The Formation and Transmission of Western Legal Culture: 150 Books That Made the Law in the Age of Printing*, ed. Serge Dauchy et al. (Cham: Springer, 2016), 129–32.

[7] Speckhan, *Single Centuria of Questions of Imperial, Pontifical and Saxon Law* 1.18. Ed. note: Eberhard Speckhan (1550–1627) was professor of law in Helmstedt.

[8] *fides publica.*

[9] Ed. note: The Constitutio Criminalis Carolina is the influential criminal law enacted by Emperor Charles V in 1532; see Peter Oestmann, "Constitutio Criminalis Carolina," in *Encyclopedia of Early Modern History Online*, http:dx.doi.org/10.1163/2352-0272_emho_SIM_018136.

Peter Prem refers to this in his book[10] on promises of security and the faith given by public authorities,[11] as does Johannes Molanus.[12]

The fathers of the Council of Constance followed the same line of thought during the sixth session: "By the present decree we offer any kind of safe conduct against violence as far as it is in our might and as far as our true faith demands it, but always without violating justice."

4. The second type of safe conduct, which is given with partial abrogation of the general law, has been dealt with by the fathers of the Council of Trent after the fifteenth session, where they say they will grant all Germans, both Catholics and heretics, "public faith and full security to come to Trent, stay there, linger and sojourn there, make proposals and discuss; in addition, they will not be punished, under the guise of religion, for crimes perpetrated against religion, whether in the past or the future." In this part they derogate from the Council of Constance, which had not allowed for such a complete security but adopted the common clause "always without violating justice."

5. Now that we have noted all this, the question remains: Should a Catholic ruler—no matter whether he belongs to the worldly or the ecclesiastical government—grant heretics safe conduct to freely arrive and return, either under general or under particular law, and should he keep his faith with them or not? All Catholic authors answer this question with an unambiguous yes. The reason for this can already be found in what I stated before. Because if neither heresy nor excommunication nor public hostility can be an objection to keeping one's faith in licit and honorable pacts, then I do not see how faith would not need to be kept when it comes to safe conduct. After Emperor Charles V had promised Martin Luther safe conduct in order to travel to Worms, he did not allow anything going against the faith he had given. What is more, when a certain prince asked him why he would not break his faith with a heretical man, he allegedly replied, "Even if

---

[10] Ed. note: Prem, *Single Book on Promises of Security and Public Faith* 7. Peter Prem (Petrus Bremus), a sixteenth-century German jurist about whom little is known, was a counselor to the dukes of Saxony.

[11] *fides publica*.

[12] Molanus, *On the Duty to Keep Faith with Heretics* 2.3.

the entire world relinquished its faith in given promises, it would still need to stand firm with the emperor." A splendid remark, and worthy of a Catholic emperor.[13]

6. At this point I am often astonished by our adversaries, who, even though they can hear us making these points, yell openly that we teach the exact opposite. They come up with the example of Jan Hus[14] and Jerome of Prague[15] and say that although they had been granted safe conduct, they were nonetheless burned at the stake at the instigation of the Council of Constance, against the faith given to them. They also add that the fathers of this council declared in articulate statements that one does not have to keep his faith with heretics. And on top of that, they pretend they were denied access to the Council of Trent themselves, even though they had been granted safe conduct. What do we do with all this? As I have said before, they are similar to the Pharisees.[16] The Pharisees had heard from Christ himself, "Render to Caesar the things that are Caesar's, and to God the things that are God's."[17] But they still dared to publicly blame him in the presence of Pilate: "We found this man misleading our nation and forbidding us to give tribute to Caesar."[18] This is exactly the way our opponents

---

[13] Molanus, *On the Duty to Keep Faith with Heretics* 1.2.

[14] Ed. note: Jan Hus (c. 1369–1415) was a major church reformer in Bohemia and former rector of Charles University in Prague. Inspired by John Wycliffe, he railed against clerical abuse and the temporal power of the church. He was executed at the Council of Constance. Ota Pavlíček, "The Chronology of the Life and Work of Jan Hus," in *A Companion to Jan Hus*, ed. Ota Pavlíček and František Šmahel (Leiden: Brill, 2015), 9–68.

[15] Ed. note: Jerome of Prague (c. 1378–1416) was a follower of Jan Hus. An alumnus of Oxford University, he played a seminal role in spreading John Wycliffe's reformist ideas in Bohemia. Thomas A. Fudge, *Jerome of Prague and the Foundations of the Hussite Movement* (Oxford: Oxford University Press, 2016).

[16] Ed. note: See Becanus's statement of the disputation question above, nos. 4–5 (pp. 8–9).

[17] Ed. note: Matt. 22:21.

[18] Ed. note: Luke 23:2.

treat us. Privately and publicly, in spoken and in written word, we teach and declare *one should keep his faith with heretics*; and still they wish to drag us unwillingly to the other side.

7. But let us take a look at what they bring forward. They say the faith given to Jan Hus has been violated. I deny this. Who violated it? The fathers of the Council of Constance? They did not even give him this faith. Emperor Sigismund?[19] Admittedly, he gave his faith, but he did not violate it, neither did the fathers. Other authors have already proved this with a variety of arguments; I will satisfy myself with only two of them. *The first argument*: someone who grants safe conduct under general law provides one with nothing more than security against unjust violence, but always with regard to justice and the execution of the law, as has been proved by the statement of the lawyers cited above. The emperor gave Jan Hus safe conduct under general law; thus, he gave nothing more than security against unjust violence; and he indeed warranted this, because Jan Hus did not suffer anything unjustly. To conclude: the emperor kept his faith with him. "But he has been burned!" they will say. Yes, I admit he has been burned—but not unjustly. First, when the emperor granted him safe conduct, he forbade him to flee on pain of death. But Hus ignored this prohibition and escaped; consequently, he could rightly be punished. Second, when he had been captured again, he refused to abjure his heresy. But the imperial laws prescribe the death penalty to persevering heretics, according to law *Quicunque*.[20] Hence, no injustice happened.

8. So what will our adversaries then say for their beloved Hus? Of course, if they want to defend him, they must deny one accusation or the other: either that he fled or that he persisted in his heresy. But they

---

[19] Ed. note: Sigismund (1368–1437), the future emperor of the Holy Roman Empire (1433–1437), granted safe conducts to Jan Hus and Jerome of Prague to attend the Council of Constance. The extent to which those safe conducts granted protection to the Bohemian reformers is still subject to debate. See Thomas A. Fudge, *The Trial of Jan Hus: Medieval Heresy and Criminal Procedure* (Oxford: Oxford University Press, 2013), 177–84.

[20] Cod. 1.5.8*pr*.

cannot deny either. All reliable sources, including Nauclerus[21] and Cochlaeus,[22] testify to his flight. Campion expressed our view most elegantly in his *Ten Reasons*, presented to academics in England: "But Hus would not have been punished at all if he had not himself enfeebled the power of the official letter given to him by Emperor Sigismund. A perfidious and pestilent man, he was caught fleeing—which Emperor Sigismund had forbidden him on pain of death. He violated all conditions he had put on paper with the emperor."[23] And even though Whitaker, the Calvinist who polemicized against Campion,[24] says he lies about the flight of Hus (as if he could change the facts by saying so), other Calvinists honestly acknowledge what happened, especially Laurence Humphrey, a theologian from Oxford, who attacked Campion in an enormous volume.[25] I tell you, this theologian admits that Hus

---

[21] Nauclerus, *Chronicle*, generation 48. Ed. note: Johannes Nauclerus (c. 1430–1510), doctor of canon law, gained fame as the founding rector of the University of Tübingen and as a humanist historian. Hubertus Seibert, "Nauclerus, Johannes," *Neue Deutsche Biographie* 18 (1997), 760–61 (online version), https://www.deutsche-biographie.de/sfz68101.html#ndbcontent.

[22] Cochlaeus, *History of the Hussites* 2. Ed. note: Johannes Cochlaeus (1479–1552) studied arts, law, and theology. Although he is often remembered for his textbook on music, Cochlaeus was actively involved in combatting the Hussites and the Lutherans. He wrote historical works on both religious groups. Heinrich Grimm, "Cochlaeus, Johannes," *Neue Deutsche Biographie* 3 (1957), 304–6 (online version), https://www.deutsche-biographie.de/sfz8542.html#ndbcontent.

[23] Campion, *Ten Reasons Proposed to His Adversaries for Disputation* 4. Ed. note: Edmund Campion (1540–1581), Jesuit theologian and martyr, was actively involved in combatting the Anglicans, to which his *Ten Reasons* was directed. He was declared saint by Pope Paul VI in 1970 and gave his name to Campion Hall at Oxford University.

[24] Ed. note: William Whitaker (1548–1595), a Calvinist theologian at the University of Cambridge, wrote several polemical works against Jesuits such as Robert Bellarmine, Thomas Stapleton, and Edmund Campion.

[25] Ed. note: Humphrey (1527–1590) was commissioned by Oxford University to refute Campion's *Ten Reasons*. See Eleanor Kathleen Merchant, "Doctissimus pater pastorum: Laurence Humphrey and Reformed Humanist

secretly ran away from Constance. But for this he has two excuses. First, he says, Hus saw he was being watched by the fathers and was subject to suspicion; therefore he took flight. Second, around the same time three popes took flight as well: John, Benedict, and Eugene. Therefore, Hus is not to blame. Yet in truth, neither of these excuses is sufficient. To begin with, the fathers kept an eye on him with good reasons, for they knew he publicly preached heretical teachings in Bohemia, and he might also spread his virus in Constance. But did he have to flee, on that account, against the faith given to him? As far as the other excuse is concerned, the guilt of one person does not provide an excuse for the guilt of another. Definitely, these popes took flight—I do not deny this. But does that mean Hus was allowed to run off and go unpunished, against all agreements that had been made? As if just because Judas was a traitor, others were allowed to be traitors as well without punishment? That is not the way it works, my friend.

9. Enough about his flight. Our opponents cannot deny the fact that Hus was a heretic. He held on to his views and pertinaciously defended the doctrine of John Wycliffe, which, among other things, consists of these points: (1) God is obliged to obey the devil. (2) If a bishop or a priest lives in mortal sin, he does not ordain, confect, baptize, or consecrate. (3) There is no civil lord, no prelate, no bishop, as long as he lives in mortal sin. (4) All things happen out of absolute necessity. (5) Oaths taken to confirm human contracts and civic commerce are illicit. (6) It goes against Holy Scripture that clergymen have possessions of their own. (7) Augustine, Benedict, and Bernard were condemned, unless they repented of having owned possessions. (8) All religious orders, without distinction, have been introduced by the devil. We can find this in the Council of Constance,[26] in Cochlaeus,[27] Sanders,[28]

Education in Mid-Tudor England" (PhD diss., Queen Mary University, 2013), 297–98, http://qmro.qmul.ac.uk/jspui/handle/123456789/8618.

[26] Council of Constance, session 8.

[27] Cochlaeus, *History of the Hussites* 1.

[28] Sanders, *On the Visible Monarchy of the Church* 7. Ed. note: Nicholas Sanders (Sanderus, c. 1530–1581) was a Catholic priest and historian who polemicized against the Anglicans. In 1565 he was appointed professor of

and others. These dogmas are clearly heretical, as even Lutherans and Calvinists must admit. To conclude: Hus was a heretic, and even a pertinacious one, who refused to abjure these points of view.

10. Enough about this first argument, from which we can conclude that it was not the emperor who violated his faith with Hus, but Hus with the emperor. *The second argument* is, if Hus's faith had been violated, beyond doubt either he himself or Jerome of Prague or definitely the Bohemians would have complained about this. But none of them have ever voiced a complaint. Who would consequently believe his faith had been violated? For sure, when Hus was led to his execution, he spoke freely, uttered many accusations against the Catholic Church, and appealed to Christ as his supreme judge, as we can read in the proceedings of his trial written by several different authors. But we do not read he said a single word about the violation of his faith. Similarly, Jerome of Prague, who was executed a few days after Hus, publicly testified Hus had been a good, just, and pious man, unworthy of such a death; but he never recalled Hus had endured anything against the faith that had been given to him. We can read about this in a letter of Poggio Bracciolini,[29] who himself had been an eyewitness of Jerome's death and later wrote about it. Poggio loved to attack the clergy, and if he had been able to brand the Catholics with this mark, he certainly would not have missed the opportunity. I also refer to the Bohemian nobility. They favored Hus enormously and defended his dogmas; but when later on they were called to the Council of Basel even without safe conduct, a significant delegation of them was present. Who would

---

theology at the University of Louvain; see Thomas Veech, *Dr Nicholas Sanders and the English Reformation (1530–1581)* (Louvain: Bureaux du Recueil, Bibliothèque de l'Université, 1935).

[29] Ed. note: After training as a lawyer, Poggio Bracciolini (1380–1459) entered the service of prelates and popes. He was an outspoken critic of clerical authority and a humanist philologist who contributed to the rediscovery of many classical texts; Bracciolini witnessed Jerome of Prague's death at the Council of Constance. He reported about it in a letter to Leonardo Bruni, which is included in English translation in Fudge, *Jerome of Prague*, 338–44.

believe this could have happened if they mistrusted Catholics because of Hus's violated faith?

11. I can conclude the same from Martin Luther, who wrote a specific article on Jan Hus, which, as other writings, was condemned by Pope Leo X. Even though he praised Hus for his piety and his doctrine (Should anyone be surprised about this?), Luther did not write anything about violated safe conduct. From all this I draw the following conclusion. If either the Catholic emperor or the fathers of the Council of Constance had acted against the faith that they had given publicly, then one of their adversaries would certainly have thrown this evidence at them. But neither Hus himself, nor Jerome of Prague, nor the Bohemian nobility, nor Luther—all of them enemies of the Catholics—used this against them. This is a clear sign that nothing of this kind happened.

12. I have spoken sufficiently about Hus. Now I come to the case of Jerome of Prague. This is what we know for sure about him. (1) He refused safe conduct from Emperor Sigismund (as Cochlaeus,[30] Molanus,[31] and others have written). (2) He was nonetheless summoned by the Council of Constance, which granted him conditional safe conduct—namely, "always without violation of justice." We can find this in the sixth session of this council and at various places of other authors. (3) After citation, he appeared, entered into a discussion, was convicted, and abjured his heresy. This is evident from session 19 of the same council, where we find the formula used for the abjuration of his heresy. (4) He then slipped back into heresy, took flight, was caught, and then was burned on the stake, as we can read in session 21 of the council and in Cochlaeus, Molanus, Campion, and others. From this I conclude that his faith has not been violated, first because he received safe conduct under the condition "always without violation of justice"; second, because he ended his own safe conduct by taking flight; and third, because he slipped back into the heresy he had just abjured.

---

[30] Cochlaeus, *History of the Hussites* 2.

[31] Molanus, *On the Duty to Keep Faith with Heretics* 3.2.

13. The only thing left is the last part of the objection, in which our adversaries claim the fathers of the Council of Constance decided one should not keep his faith with heretics. However, this is a plain lie. These are the words of the council:

> This holy synod declares that a safe conduct granted by the emperor, the kings, and other secular rulers to heretics and those defamed by heresy cannot be the source of prejudice to the Catholic faith or ecclesiastical jurisdiction. It declares that such safe conduct can and must not hinder that a competent ecclesiastical judge lawfully inquires about the errors of those persons and launches the other procedures against them in the appropriate way. He should not be hindered to go on and punish those persons according to the requirements of justice when they pertinaciously refuse to renounce their errors, despite the fact that they were relying on a safe conduct to come to the trial and would otherwise have refrained from doing so. The synod declares that the one who promised the safe conduct does not, by virtue of this, incur any obligation, as long as he did what lay in his power to protect the persons summoned to the trial.[32]

These are the words of the Council of Constance that are the basis of our adversaries' claim that one should not keep his faith with heretics. But who does not see they are either mistaken or simply making a false accusation? The fathers of the council laid down two decrees through their statement. The first decree is that secular power may in no way impede the lawful exercise of ecclesiastical power. If a secular prince grants a certain heretic safe conduct, this may not hinder an ecclesiastical judge to do his job. He must be able to examine the defendant and proceed according to the available charges and proofs against him. What kind of fault can be found in this decree? Nothing at all. For it is most abiding to both law and reason, as I will demonstrate as follows. When there are two rulers with different jurisdictional powers and tribunals and one of them is more powerful and superior to the

---

[32] Council of Constance, session 19.

other, the inferior ruler may not hinder the superior in the execution of his jurisdiction. Accordingly, the safety the inferior ruler has granted does not extend to the tribunal of the superior ruler because "a superior is not bound by the laws and agreements of an inferior," as the canon law stipulates.[33] A secular and an ecclesiastical ruler have different tribunals, with the ecclesiastical tribunal being superior.[34] Consequently, when a secular ruler grants one of his subjects safe conduct, he may not extend this to the tribunal of his superior without his consent; neither may he impede the jurisdiction of the superior ruler by the safety he has given. What could be clearer? Legal experts deal with the same matter in a most eloquent way. Eberhard Speckhan, for example, writes about it as follows: "A superior judge is not bound to ratify the faith of an inferior judge, since it is in the interest of the state that crimes are punished and since the superior judge cannot be bound by the laws and agreements of his inferior."[35]

14. The second decree laid down by the council is that a secular ruler who promised someone security does not incur any further obligation as long as he did what lay in his power to protect that person. Who could doubt this? A person who promised a safe conduct cannot be considered to have promised more than what he was capable of. So if he does what lies in his power, he does not violate his word—namely, the faith he gave through his promise. These are the two decrees of the Council of Constance. The council does not deny through them that one should keep his faith with heretics, as our adversaries viciously raise against us. Rather, it teaches secular rulers what their obligations with regard to safe conduct are, and how far their power and jurisdiction reach when granting and promising safety.

---

[33] Dec. Greg. 1.33.16.

[34] Dec. Greg. 1.33.6.

[35] Speckhan, *Single Centuria* 1.18.

Appendix

Addressing the False Claims Made in the Little Book *Third Defense of the Federated States of Lower Germany against the Calumnious Reproach That We Are Disturbing the Peace*

Recently, a Calvinist book by an unknown author appeared titled *Third Defense of the Federated States of Lower Germany against the Calumnious Reproach That We Are Disturbing the Peace and Are Entirely Rejecting It*. In this book the author (whoever it may be)[1] tries to prove two points. The first is that not the federated states but the Spanish are to blame for the fact that thus far, peace has not been established in Belgium. The main reason he gives is that all peace treaties concluded on different occasions until now have been accepted by the federated states of lower Germany but have been treacherously violated and broken by the Spanish. His second point is that we may not even hope for peace anymore in the future for a variety of obstacles on the part of the Spanish, even if the federated states are utterly inclined to make peace. These are the alleged obstacles the anonymous author lists:

1. The Spanish persist in their idolatry and tyranny.
2. The king of Spain and the archdukes, Albert and Isabella, have sworn that they were not intent on tolerating heretics in their kingdom and provinces.

---

[1] Ed. note: Pieter Cornelis van Brederode (ca. 1559–1637), a Calvinist jurist and Dutch ambassador to the Holy Roman Empire, has been designated by Tobias Dienst and Christoph Strohm as the most likely author of this anonymous pamphlet; see their introduction to this translation.

3. They consider the federated states of lower Germany as heretics and at the same time declare that *one should not keep his faith with heretics.*
4. They accuse the federated states of lower Germany of the crime of rebellion.
5. The end and scope of peace with Spain would be nothing but the extermination of heretics.

This is the summary of his book. My goal is not to refute each of these points individually (there will be others able to do this extensively) but merely those points that seem to relate to our topic—namely, keeping faith with heretics. And to avoid being tedious or boring, I will limit myself to refuting the following selected propositions:

1. Catholics teach one should not keep his faith with heretics.
2. Catholics do not keep their faith with heretics in practice; they continuously act against agreements made and sworn on.
3. Catholics rescind all their agreements and promises made to heretics whenever they see fit by asking for papal dispensation.
4. Catholics violate all their agreements and promises made to heretics through the use of equivocations characteristic of the Jesuits.
5. Catholics are worse than Turks; and one should much less enter into a peace treaty with Catholics than with Turks, first, because they do not keep their faith; second, because they are enemies of God; third, because they do not want to grant freedom of religion; fourth, because they want to protect the Apostolic See; sixth, because they swear obedience to the pope.
6. The king of Spain is a notorious heretic, and he must be expelled from his Catholic kingdom by all Evangelical forces combined.
7. Emperor Sigismund said he was not bound to keep his promises with Jan Hus and Jerome of Prague, contrary to what he had promised to the pope before.

There are many more and even more absurd propositions in that same little book, but I will let those pass because they are not relevant to my purpose. So now I will briefly examine this limited set of propositions.

Examination of the First Proposition by the Anonymous Calvinist Author

Now I will finally deal with you, my friend, whoever you are. You say that Catholics teach and have decided at three different councils—those of the Lateran, Constance, and Trent—that one should not keep his faith with heretics. This is, to put it very mildly, a blatant lie. Catholics neither teach this nor did the councils decide anything like that. I have shown this elaborately in my treatise *On the Duty to Keep Faith with Heretics*. But to make even clearer how big your lie is, let us take a quick look at what the councils you mention actually said. In the Lateran Council, which was held successively under Popes Julius II and Leo X, I do not find anything else than the fact that the sixth session grants safe conduct to come to Rome to the council to all, *except to schismatics and others who were prohibited to attend by general law*. Yet from this you conclude it has been decided one should not keep his faith with heretics? Nothing could be further from the truth. It is one thing to deny schismatics or heretics safe conduct, but quite another to decide one should not keep his faith once safe conduct has been granted to them. About the Council of Constance I spoke sufficiently in chapter 12 of my treatise. And from the Council of Trent you should have drawn the exact opposite conclusion than you did. For in session 15 it gives not only Catholics but even heretics "public faith and full security to come to Trent, stay there, linger and sojourn there, make proposals and discuss; in addition, they will not be punished, under the guise of religion, for crimes perpetrated against religion, whether in the past or the future." Who of sound mind could say that these words declare one should not keep his faith with heretics?

APPENDIX

Examination of the Second Proposition

You say that in practice Catholics do not keep their faith with heretics. You try to prove this point by first saying that the archdukes of Upper Austria, against the agreements they made and swore upon, restored the Catholic Mass, threw out the Evangelicals (that is to say, the Lutherans and Calvinists), and admitted the Jesuits instead. Your second argument is that all peace treatises in Belgium were accepted by the federated states of lower Germany but were always treacherously broken by the Spanish.

First, I reply by saying that I do not defend all the practical actions of all Catholics, but solely the Catholic doctrine.

Second, how do you know the archdukes of Austria did this against the agreements they had sworn? Definitely they acted against the wishes of the Calvinists, who hate Catholic Masses and Jesuits. But you will not easily convince me that they also acted against their given faith. If they are Catholics and deeply loyal to the Holy See, as you both acknowledge and regret, how could you imagine that they would suddenly turn so oblivious to their original declaration of faith that they would spontaneously agree to keep in the Calvinists while eliminating Catholics? You are mistaken, my friend, if you believe this.

Concerning the Spanish, I will condemn you with your own words. In that very same book, you write that twenty-four years ago, the federated states of lower Germany, by a decree of all Belgian estates, abjured the Spanish empire for eternity and that accordingly, from that time on, they neither wanted nor were able to negotiate or come to a peace agreement with the Spanish. Based on this I ask you, Why did the federated states agree to negotiate about a peace treaty if twenty-four years ago they had actually sworn that they did not want to negotiate a peace agreement with the Spanish? Either the federated states have committed perjury, or you are a liar. And I also ask you this: How could these peace negotiations have been abruptly broken off by the Spanish if no negotiations for peace were started up with them? Leave me alone with your lies.

Examination of the Third Proposition

You say that Catholics rescind all their agreements and promises made to heretics by obtaining a dispensation from the pope. These are your words: "The fourth reason is papal dispensation—and given the existence of this remedy, how can one possibly defend himself against such criminal behavior. Papal dispensation reduces all contracts to nothing, whether concluded by kings, princes, or entire peoples, as soon as they are deemed hostile to the interests of the Catholic Church." There is no need to be so afraid of that crime. The pope does not rescind contracts of princes and kings according to his arbitrary wishes, as you think. Let me explain this to you.

Contracts between Catholics and heretics can be of two different kinds: some deal with faith, religion, and ecclesiastical matters; others with civil and secular matters. If Catholic kings or princes conclude a contract with heretics in a matter of faith, religion, or ecclesiastical matters, they can do so with or without the pope's knowledge. If the pope does not know about the contract at the moment of its conclusion, he may, as soon as he learns about it, confirm the contract if it is good or declare it invalid if it is bad. Every leader, after all, is allowed to do so with his subjects in matters for which he is competent. If he knows of the contract beforehand and agrees on it, he may not rescind it later according to his own arbitrary wishes unless some new circumstance intervenes. This may occur in any contract. I spoke about this above.[2]

But if Catholic kings and princes bargain with heretics in civil and secular matters, and if these agreements are otherwise honest and valid according to civil law, the pope may not rescind them as he pleases and may not reduce them to nothing. For even though he holds supreme ecclesiastical power and ecclesiastical jurisdiction over the entire Christian world, he does not have civil and temporal supreme power, except in certain provinces and city states that are subjected to him like to a secular prince.

Someone might object: the pope lays claim to all power Christ ever possessed since he proclaims that he is the vicar of Christ on earth.

---

[2] *On the Duty to Keep Faith with Heretics* 7.2.

And Christ did not merely possess ecclesiastical power but also political power in the entire world, according to this verse in the gospel of Matthew: "All authority in heaven and on earth has been given to me" (28:18). Hence, the pope claims for himself both supreme ecclesiastical and civil power over the Christian world. To this objection I reply that according to his human nature, Christ did not hold any dominion or temporal jurisdiction over this world, as he himself admitted in the gospel of John: "My kingdom is not of this world" (18:36). And the pope does not claim more for himself than what Christ granted to him.

So why does he sometimes manage civil affairs? Why did Pope Nicholas write in his letter to Michael, "Christ entrusted to St. Peter, who bears the keys of the eternal life, the jurisdiction over both earth and heaven"?[3] Why did Boniface VIII in his papal bull *Unam sanctam* declare the pope was to have two swords,[4] according to this word of Luke: "Look, Lord, here are two swords" (22:38)? And finally, why did the canon laws provide that judging lawsuits, both spiritual and temporal, belongs to the competence of the pope?[5]

I will reply to these points individually. In advance, I wish to state that the pope, inasmuch as he is the vicar of Christ on earth, does not directly possess any temporal jurisdiction according to divine law; he does so only indirectly. The former part of this statement is true because even Christ himself did not possess this jurisdiction directly in accordance with his human nature. The latter part can be explained in the following way. The pope has direct supreme power and spiritual jurisdiction over all Christians, even over kings and princes, based on this word of Christ: "Feed my sheep."[6] The goal of this jurisdiction, however, is the spiritual good of the militant church and of all Christians. Therefore the pope has the right to govern the

---

[3] Ed. note: Pope Nicholas I to Emperor Michael III. The authenticity of this passage is unclear. In the Friedberg edition of Gratian's *Decretum* (Dist.22 c.1), the passage is attributed to a letter written by Pope Nicholas II to the Christians of Milan. Compare Becanus's comments further on.

[4] *Extravagantes communes* 1.8.1.

[5] Dec. Grat. C.11 q.1 c.7 and c.35.

[6] Ed. note: John 21:17.

church and all Christians inasmuch as that is necessary for the spiritual good of the entire community. Thus, on the basis of this right he may even, albeit indirectly, make decisions on temporal matters when the common good requires so. This is nothing other than having secular power indirectly.[7]

From this fundamental principle it easily becomes clear when and to what extent the pope may grant dispensation in civil contracts concluded by Christian princes and kings. He may not do this without urgent necessity of the spiritual good. This is the meaning of the passage in Paul's second letter to the Corinthians: "according to the power which the Lord has given me for edification and not for destruction" (13:10). From this passage I infer the following: the pope and other prelates of the church have been given all ecclesiastical power "for edification" and not "for destruction." If a pope decided to use his dispensatory power over agreements and contracts concluded by secular princes without any urgent necessity of the spiritual good, he would use it "for destruction" and not "for edification" because he would provide an occasion to violate contractual faith without a legitimate reason. Therefore, he does not have divine power to do this. As Domingo de Soto rightly pointed out in his treatise *On Justice and Right*: "The pope may not dissolve an oath to the disadvantage of the person whose interests are at stake."[8]

Moreover, the words attributed to Pope Nicholas cannot actually be found in his letters, although they are quoted by Gratian.[9] And even if these words are truly his, they must be understood as follows: Christ entrusted Peter the right to governance in heaven and on earth—that is, the power to bind in heaven and on earth according to the words in the gospel of Matthew: "I will give you the keys of the kingdom of heaven, and whatever you bind on earth shall be bound in heaven"

---

[7] Ed. note: On Becanus's reception of Bellarmine's theory of the indirect secular power of the church, see Stefania Tutino, *Empire of Souls: Robert Bellarmine and the Christian Commonwealth* (Oxford: Oxford University Press, 2010), 211–60.

[8] Soto, *On Justice and Right* 8.1.9.

[9] Dec. Grat. Dist.22 c.1. Ed. note: See n. 3 above.

(16:19). The words of Nicholas cannot be understood in a different way; otherwise, he would contradict himself. For in his letter to Michael he eloquently explains that Christ has made a distinction between the offices of the pope and the emperor to prevent the emperor from seizing the rights of the pope or vice versa.

Regarding the two swords mentioned by Luke—"Look, Lord, here are two swords" (22:38)—this reference has nothing to do with our argument. The saying, after all, does not concern the spiritual and temporal sword here, but swords in the literal sense of the word. Christ had spoken: "And let the one who has no sword sell his cloak and buy one." And his disciples replied: "Look, Lord, here are two swords." But Christ spoke about a real sword. He wanted to indicate that not much later the fear and trepidation of the apostles would become as great as of those people who sell their tunic in order to buy a sword to defend themselves. Therefore, this is the literal meaning of the word. Boniface interprets it mystically to concern spiritual power, which the pope has directly, and temporal power, which he has indirectly.

The canon laws quoted here prove nothing at all. The first is the one by Emperor Theodosius, who—out of piety, not because he had to—transferred this power to the pope and the other bishops so that they could pass judgment in civil cases brought before them. But now this canon law has been abrogated, as the gloss in the same place asserts. The second one is of uncertain origin, and therefore it is indicated as a *palea*.[10] Nevertheless, it can still be explained in the following way: all civil lawsuits that cannot be resolved by secular judges will be left to the judgment of the church through the procedure of fraternal correction, as Pope Innocent III teaches in canon *Novit ille*.[11] For when

---

[10] Ed. note: The word *palea* designates passages in Gratian's *Decretum* that have probably been added at a later stage. They are often attributed to an early commentator of the *Decretum* who is known as Paucapalea. A famous example of a *palea* is the *Palea Constantinus* (Dist. 96 c. 14), which inserted the story of the Donation of Constantine—used as legitimation for the church's jurisdictional power—into Gratian's *Decretum*. See Johannes Fried, *Donation of Constantine and Constitutum Constantini* (Berlin: De Gruyter, 2007), 19.

[11] Dec. Greg. 2.1.13.

a secular judge refuses to pass judgment or one of the parties to the dispute does not want to comply with the law, one must take recourse to an ecclesiastical judge. The ecclesiastical judge must remind the judge and the party of their respective duties and excommunicate them if they remain contumacious.[12]

I have explained these things quite elaborately to soothe you about the effects of papal dispensation that you seem to fear so much. You can be reassured. His dispensation is not used "for destruction," just "for edification."[13]

Examination of the Fourth Proposition

You say that Catholics violate all their agreements and promises made to heretics through the use of "Jesuitical equivocations," and you try to prove this through the following example: Even if a peace agreement has been concluded between Catholics and heretics, the Catholics will, without any further objection, still persecute the heretics and try to exterminate them in every way possible. Then they say they do not go against their own agreements because the established peace is not ecclesiastical but merely political in nature and has not been made with heretics inasmuch as they are heretics, but inasmuch as they are humans or citizens. Therefore, it is allowed to persecute and extirpate them inasmuch as they are heretics. That leaves the civil peace untouched.

First, I would like to ask you this: Why do you call this art of deceiving "Jesuitical equivocation"? I suspect you are doing just the same as the other preachers of your sect. Despite knowing better, they openly yell from their lecterns that the Jesuits are the archfathers and architects of any fraud and wrongdoing in the world. And no doubt: if they go

---

[12] Ed. note: On the competence of ecclesiastical courts in cases of inadequacy of secular justice (*ex defectu justitiae*), see Richard H. Helmholz, *The Spirit of Classical Canon Law* (Athens: University of Georgia Press, 1996), 132–44.

[13] Ed. note: Becanus is repeating the terminology of 2 Cor. 13:10, which he cited above.

on like this, they will soon convince the people that the Jesuits introduced original sin in this world and that the Jesuits were the ones who by secret confession gave the advice to Absalom to inflict war on his father David! Indeed, not so long ago, you Calvinists spread rumors like this. Allegedly, Jesuit monks in Bavaria raped a girl, and, as if that were not yet enough, they were also said to have committed an atrocious murder. I think you and your preachers must be dreaming up these things. But let us move past this now.

Jesuits do not teach or allow lying or deceiving others through equivocations. They teach what Catholics have always taught up until now: in any human gathering, in all contracts and promises, one ought to act sincerely, honestly, and without any feigning or equivocation.[14] You behave badly if you keep one thing secret in your mind but say quite another in words. However, when the circumstances demand so, you may wisely use silence or dissimulation, but if you wish to speak, you should do so without lying, without deceit, without fraud.

There is one case, though, that has given rise to debate among the Jesuits but also among other theologians. This case is whether an accused person, when being interrogated in court about his crime, may deny it or respond in ambiguous fashion. In this case they make a distinction: If the judge interrogates the defendant following the procedures and in full regard of the rule of law,[15] the accused is bound to speak the truth. But when the trial does not comply with the procedures—namely, with the rule of law—he is not. This is the opinion of

---

[14] Ed. note: For an overview of early modern Catholic doctrine on this point, see Stefania Tutino, "Nothing But the Truth? Hermeneutics and Morality in the Doctrines of Equivocation and Mental Reservation in Early Modern Europe," *Renaissance Quarterly* 64, no. 1 (2011): 115–55.

[15] *ordo iuris*. Ed. note: on the canon law origins of modern conceptions of procedural fairness and "rule of law," see Kenneth Pennington, "The Jurisprudence of Procedure," in *The History of Courts and Procedure in Medieval Canon Law*, ed. Wilfried Hartmann and Kenneth Pennington (Washington, DC: Catholic University of America Press, 2016), 125–59.

Henry of Ghent,[16] Sylvester,[17] Angelo,[18] Dr. Navarrus,[19] St. Thomas,[20] and others at many different places. We can also gather this from the canon law, particularly from several canons in title *De accusationibus* in Pope Gregory IX's Decretals.[21] The reason for the former is that everyone is obliged to obey a superior who gives legitimate orders, and the superior gives orders legitimately when he interrogates the accused according to the rule of law. So in that case the accused is bound to obey by speaking the truth. The reason for the latter is that a judge does not have the right to interrogate unless he follows the rule of law. Therefore, if he does not follow the rule of law, he may not impose any obligation on the accused to reveal his crime, for the law does not grant him this power. The judge is considered not to follow the rule of law when he interrogates about a hidden crime of which there is no rumor against the accused, no adequate evidence or not even half proof.

So what should the accused do in such a case in which he is not bound to confess the crime he committed? St. Thomas provides us with an answer at the place cited before, saying he may "try to escape by making an appeal or in another licit way, but he may not tell a lie." But what if he simply denies he committed the crime—will he be a liar? Some authors think he may deny this without any lie involved as long as the crime is hidden. The reason is that a judge cannot pos-

---

[16] Henry of Ghent, *Quodlibeta* 1.34. Ed. note: Henry of Ghent (d. 1293) was one of the most important theologians at the University of Paris in the late thirteenth century.

[17] Sylvester, *Summa silvestrina*, s.v. "confessio delicti," q. 1.

[18] Angelo, *Summa angelica*, s.v. "confessio delicti," q. 1. Ed. note: Angelo Carletti de Chivasso (c. 1414–1495), a former professor of law at the University of Bologna and a magistrate, entered the Franciscan order later in life. His manual for confessors served as a major source of inspiration for Sylvester and became very influential among the theologians of the School of Salamanca.

[19] Dr. Navarrus, *Enchiridion or Manual for Confessors and Penitents* 25.53.

[20] Thomas Aquinas, *Summa theologiae* II.2, Q. 69, A. 1.

[21] Dec. Greg. 5.1.17 (*Qualiter et quando*); Dec. Greg. 5.1.19 (*Cum oporteat*); Dec. Greg. 5.1.21 (*Inquisitionis*).

sibly prepare for an interrogation about a crime that has not become generally known in some way or another. To conclude, if the accused denies he committed such a crime, he does not lie as long as the crime is still hidden.

A similar question often arises regarding a judge who publicly and "according to the charges and available evidence"[22] convicts an accused person whom he privately knows to be innocent. Should we say this judge lies when he openly announces someone to be a criminal who in reality is not? Most authors deny this.[23] The reason for this is that he does not proclaim anything other than what he must proclaim "according to the charges and available evidence." Therefore, because the accused is now a criminal by public charge and evidence—even though he is not before God—the judge can without any lie announce he is a criminal.

This is the view of the experts on the way the defendant can act during interrogation in a legal procedure. If this view is true, then how can you accuse them falsely? If this view is erroneous, then point out the mistake. You, however, are shameless: you wish to extend what has only been said about the rights of defendants in lawsuits to others as well.

Examination of the Fifth Proposition

You say that Catholics are worse than Turks, and one should much less enter into a peace treaty with Catholics than with Turks. Obviously,

---

[22] *secundum allegata et probata.*

[23] Ed. note: Anticipating the modern principle that "justice must not only be done, it must also be seen to be done," early modern scholastics were mostly of the opinion, indeed, that the judge should base his judgment only on information that was publicly available. Jesuits such as Lessius, however, considered that a judge in a supreme court with private knowledge about the innocence of the accused should do everything in his power to help the defendant escape the sentence by extrajudicial means. See Wim Decock, "The Judge's Conscience and the Protection of the Criminal Defendant: Moral Safeguards against Judicial Arbitrariness," in *From the Judge's Arbitrium to the Legality Principle*, ed. G. Martyn, A. Musson, and H. Pihlajamäki (Berlin: Duncker & Humblot, 2013), 69–94.

here you reveal that Calvinists are more attracted by the doctrine and companionship of the Turks than to those of the Catholics. That author who coined the term *Calvinoturcism* was right about you after all.[24]

But honestly, what do you have against Catholics? Why do you rank them even lower than Turks? Because they do not keep their faith? That is untrue. Because they are enemies of God? Not the Catholics, but the Turks are enemies of God. Or because they do not want to grant freedom of religion? You do not grant it either in England, Holland, and Frisia. Because they defend the Apostolic See? Constantine the Great, Charlemagne, and Charles V did the same, just as our Emperor Rudolph. Or because they swear obedience to the pope? Obeying is the mark of true sons; resisting is rebellion.

Examination of the Sixth Proposition

You say the king of Spain is a notorious heretic and must be expelled from his Catholic kingdom by all Evangelical forces combined. A more modest attitude would do you good, my friend. You are not just being injurious toward the king but even to the emperor. Both share the same faith. So by necessity, either neither or both of them must be heretics to you. Get yourself together. Why do you call him a "notorious heretic"? Has not he been named "Catholic King" for many centuries already? And I hope he will be named this forever. But what is this Catholic kingdom you wish to expel him from? The Spanish, of course. But if this is Catholic territory—which it certainly is—how could its king be a heretic since he adheres to the faith of this Catholic kingdom? And why do you wish to expel him by force—I thought you were a lover of peace, not of war, and I thought you wanted to encourage your Evangelicals to show more clemency and not to take up arms to

---

[24] Ed. note: Probably Becanus is referring to William Rainolds and William Gifford, who use the term *Calvinoturcism* throughout their work *Calvinoturcismus, id est Calvinisticae perfidiae cum Mahumetana collatio et dilucida utriusque sectae confutatio* (Antwerp, 1597). See M. E. H. N. Mout, "Calvinoturcisme in de zeventiende eeuw: Comenius, Leidse oriëntalisten en de Turkse Bijbel," *Tijdschrift voor Geschiedenis* 91 (1978): 576–607.

destroy kingdoms. But what you are writing here is plain rebellion. They do not want to obey their kings, and so they prepare their death.

Examination of the Seventh Proposition

You write that Emperor Sigismund said he was not bound to keep his promises to Jan Hus and Jerome of Prague, contrary to what he had promised to the pope before. In every respect you are a liar. Sigismund promised nothing to Jerome of Prague. He promised Hus safe conduct, but under this condition: that he would not flee. But Hus fled, against the agreement made. Consequently, he was rightfully punished.[25]

---

[25] See what I wrote above in *On the Duty to Keep Faith with Heretics* 12.7–8.

Index

Abraham, 80
Absalom, 114
adultery, 73–75
agreements, xxxix–xl, 11–12, 15
   with heretics, 54, 109–110, 111–12
   political, xii–xiv, xii–xiv, 5, 8, 105–6
   See also contracts
Albert and Isabella of Spain, 105
Ambrose of Milan, xxxix, 5, 35, 82–83, 90
Ammianus, 80
Angelo Carletti de Chivasso (c. 1414–1495), 115
Anglicans, ix, xxx, 98n23, 99n28
anti-Jesuit literature, xxv–xxvi, xxvii, 113–14
Antonine of Florence (1389–1459), 44, 63
Aquinas, Thomas. *See* Thomas Aquinas
Aragón, Pedro de (Petrus Aragonensis, c. 1545–1592), 31
Arcadius, Emperor, 67, 84–85
Aristophanes, 4
Arius, Arians, 79, 81, 82–83, 84–85
Athaliah, Queen, xxxn68

Augustine, xvii, xxxix, 7, 35, 99
   on heretics, 68, 79, 85–86, 90
   on lies, 39–40, 41–44
Austria, xvii, xxix–xxx, xxxi, xxxii, 108
Azor, Juan (1536–1603), 69
Azpilcueta, Martín de (1492–1586), Dr. Navarrus, 19, 44, 46, 52, 69, 71, 115

bargains (*conventio*), xl, 8, 52, 54–55, 109
Baronio, Cesare (1538–1607), 82
Bartolus of Sassoferrato (c. 1313–c. 1358), 24
Bavaria, xxx, 114
Becanus, Martinus (1563–1624), ix–x
Brederode, Pieter Cornelis van
   and, xx–xxiv, xxxv, 105
   De fide haereticis servanda, x–xiv, xx–xxiv
   Disputatio theologica de fide haereticis servanda, xiv–xv
   Manuale controversiarum huius temporis, ix–x, xivn16, xx, xxxii, xxxv

119

Index

Pareus, David and, xxvi–xxix, xxxv
  Rome, relationship with, xxx–xxxiv, xxxv
Bede the Venerable, 72
Belgium, 54, 80, 105, 108
Bellarmine, Robert (1542–1621), xiv, xv, xxx, xxxi, xxxii, xxxv, 72, 74
Belleperche, Pierre de (Petrus Bellapertica, c. 1247–1308), 23
Bible, xii, 48
  divine law, xvi, xvii, xxviii–xxix, 15, 38, 40–42, 46–47, 55, 110
  faithlessness, 46–47, 55
  heretics, avoiding, 61–62, 64
  marriage, 73–74
  pagans and idolaters, avoiding, 53–54, 55–56
Bohemia, xxx, 79, 99, 100–101
  Hus, Jan (1369–1415), xiii, 96, 97–101, 106, 118
  Jerome of Prague (c. 1378–1416), 96, 100, 101–3, 106, 118
Boniface VIII, Pope, 20, 110, 112
Bracciolini, Poggio (1380–1459), 100
Brederode, Pieter Cornelis van (ca. 1559–1637), xiv, xxi–xxiv, 105

Cajetan, Cardinal (Tommaso de Vio, 1469–1534), 34, 52, 63, 86
Calvinists, xii–xiii, xxiii, xxxi, 62, 79–80, 98, 100
  Brederode, Pieter Cornelis van (ca. 1559–1637), xiv, xxi–xxiv, 105
  Catholics and, 105, 108, 114, 117
  Plancius, Daniel (ca. 1580–1618), xii–xiii
  Whitaker, William (1548–1595), 98

Calvin, John, 15, 54
Campion, Edmund (1540–1581), 98, 101
canon law, xii, xx, xxiii, 22, 46, 49, 102–3, 110, 112
  Decretum Gratiani, 15, 48, 67, 86, 90, 110, 111
  Extravagantes communes, 110
  force and fear, 20, 23–24
  on heretics, 62, 64–68
  Liber Extra, 18, 19, 22–24, 28, 45, 65, 67, 103, 112, 115
  Liber Sextus, 15n12, 20, 28, 52n2, 62, 65, 90
Cassian, John, 41
Castellio, Sebastian, xxxvi
Castile, kingdom of, 29–30, 45
Catholic Church, 102, 109–12
  contracts with heretics, xxxv, xxxvii, 52–53, 109
  converting heretics, 42–43
  faith, keeping, 8–9, 55–59, 106, 107
  freedom of religion, xvii, xix, xxvii, 77–78, 106, 117
  jurisdiction, judges, 30, 102–3, 109–10, 112–13
  peace treaties, 106, 116–17
  regicide, xxiv, xxx–xxxi
  religious tolerance, xiv–xvi, xviii–xix, xxiii–xxiv, xxxv–xxxvi
  See also canon law
Catholic princes, political leaders, 30–32, 102–3
  agreements, contracts with heretics, 54, 109–110, 111–12
  freedom of religion, 80–85, 89
  safe conduct, 95–96, 118
  tolerance of heretics, xvii, xxxiii–xxxiv, xxxv
  waging war with heretics, 89–91

Index

Charlemagne, 81–82, 117
Charles V, Emperor, 95–96, 117
Cicero, 4, 5, 7
civil law, 16, 19, 68
   Roman, xi, 12n8, 14–15, 20, 23, 25, 81–82
   See also Justinian legal codes
civil power, of popes, 110–13
Clement VIII, Pope, 82n8
Cochlaeus, Johannes (1479–1552), 98, 99, 101
coercion, 13, 17–19, 29, 91
confessionalism, xxxvi–xxxvii
conscience, 7, 16, 25, 45–46, 54, 65
Constantine the Great, 81, 117
Constitutio Criminalis Carolina, 94
contracts (*contractus*), x–xiii, xvi, xl, xxii, 48
   Catholics and heretics, xxxv, xxxvii, 54, 62, 64, 109, 109–110, 111–12
   deceit, 19, 21–25, 56
   divine law, xxviii–xxix
   with excommunicated, 65–66
   fear and, 17–20
   Jesuits, xxv–xxvi, 106, 113–16
   Joshua and Gibeonites, xii, 55–56, 91
   Justinian legal codes, 12n8, 15, 22, 25
   marriage, xx, 18, 71–75
   mistakes, 19, 21, 23–25, 46
   onerous, 18–19, 20, 22, 24, 33–34, 48
   papal dispensations and, 109–11
   positive law, 18–19, 25–26
   Roman law, xin6, 20, 23, 25
   stipulations, 11–12, 22–23, 45–46
Council of Basel (1431–1449), 100–101

Council of Constance (1414–1418), xiii, 63, 95, 107
   Hus, Jan and, 96, 97–101
   Jerome of Prague and, 96, 100, 101–3
Council, Fifth Lateran (1512–1517), 107
Council of Nicaea (325), 81
Council of Trent (1545–1563), xiin11, 29, 74, 95, 96, 107
Council of Trullo (691), 72
Covarrubias, Diego de, y Leyva (1512–1577), 23, 24, 46

David, King, 56–57, 114
deals (*conventum*), dealing with, xl, 7–8, 14n3, 53, 55, 62, 65–66, 107
death penalty, xix, 67–68, 97, 100
deceit, deception, 38–39, 42, 91, 114
   contracts, 19, 21–25, 56
De fide haereticis servanda, x–xiv, xx–xxiv
devil, the, 40–41, 99
dispensations, 30–32, 106, 109–13
Disputatio theologica de fide haereticis servanda, xiv–xv
divine law, xvi, xvii, xxviii–xxix, 15, 110
   faithlessness, 46–47, 55
   heretics, avoiding, 61–62, 64
donations, 12, 20, 24, 48, 65, 69
Donatists, xvii, xxviii, 79, 85–86
Duhr, Bernhard (1852–1930), xv

early modern Europe, tolerance, x, xiv–xv, xxxvi–xxxviii
ecclesiastical, 67, 95
   jurisdiction, judges, 30, 102–3, 109–10, 112–13

121

law, 62, 64
power, 102, 109–11
Eleazar (Jewish martyr), 54
enemies, 89–91
England, 80, 117
    Anglicans, ix, xxx, 98n23, 99n28
    James I, ix, xxx
    Oath of Allegiance, ix, xivn16, xxiiin40, xxx
Enlightenment, xxxvi
Erasmus, xxxiv
Erstenberger, Andreas (d. 1592), xviii
Euripides, 4
Eusebius of Caesarea, 81
evil (*malum*), xl, 15, 55
    greater, xvii–xix, xxvii, xxviii, xxx, xxxii, 86
    lies as, 42–43
excommunicated, the, xx, 18
    avoiding, 61–63, 65–66
    contracts with, 62, 65–66
    keeping faith with, 64–66
    by name, xx, 63, 64–65, 66–67
    property rights, 66–69
exile, 67, 81
experts, legal, (*doctores*), xl, 7, 72, 103, 116
    contracts, 11–12, 22, 46, 66

faith (*fides*), 7–8, 22–23
    fidelity, virtue of, 33, 34–35, 44–47, 90
    unity of the, 78–79, 80–83, 85–87
faith, keeping, 3–6
    Catholics with heretics, 8–9, 55–59, 106, 107
    the excommunicated, 64–66
    God and, 56–58
    governance and, 4–5
    with heretics, x–xii, xvi, 6, 8–9, 87
    safe conduct, 93–98, 100–103, 107, 118
    in treaties, political agreements, xii–xiv, xii–xiv, 5, 8, 105–6
    in wartime, 5, 89–91
faithlessness, breaking faith, 44–47, 52, 55, 56–59
Faure, Jean (Johannes Faber, c. 1275–1340), 23
fear, 17–20, 23–24, 29, 91
Ferdinand II, Emperor, xv–xvi, xxix–xxx, xxxi, xxxv
Feu, Jean (Johannes Ignaeus, d. 1549), 23
fidelity, virtue of, 33, 34–35, 44–47, 90
force, coercion, 17–19, 29, 91
Forst, Rainer, xxxvi
France, xxiv, xxx–xxxi, 3n1
    Henry IV, xxiv, 3n1
    heresy, heretics, 53–54, 80
    Paris, ix, xxxi
Frederick V of Bohemia, xxx
freedom of religion, xvi–xviii, xix, xxiii–xxiv, xxxv, 77–79, 89, 117
    Catholic Church, xvii, xix, xxvii, xxxi, 77–78, 106, 117
    Catholic princes and, 80–85, 89
    Christ and, 78–79
    Roman law, 81–82
    state, danger to, 78–85
    unity of the faith, 78–79, 80–83, 85–87
friendship, 38–39

Gainas, Commander, 84–85
Germany, xviii, xix, xxi, xxxiv, 95
    Hanau, xxiii
    Heidelberg, ix, xiii, xxvi

heresy, heretics, 53–54, 64, 66, 69
  lower, 105–6, 108
  Mainz, ix–x, xiii–xiv, xviii
Gibeonites, xii, 55–57, 91
God, 38, 40
  keeping faith, 56–58
  oaths and, 27–28, 30, 31, 35, 48–49, 56
Gómez, Antonio (c. 1501–1561), xi, 14, 46
good, xxxi–xxxiii, xxxv, 22–23, 86, 111
gratuitous promises, 9, 12, 13–16, 24, 33–34, 49
Gregory of Valencia (1549–1603), xvii, 69, 71, 74, 86
Gregory VII, Pope, 67
Gregory IX, Pope, 115

Hanau, xxiii
Heidelberg, ix, xiii, xxvi
Henríquez, Enrique (1546–1608), 63
Henry IV of France, xxiv, 3n1
Henry of Ghent (d. 1293), 115
heretics, xix, xxviii, 61–62, 77
  arrogance, 80–81, 84–85
  avoiding, 61–62, 64, 65–66
  contracts with, xxxv, xxxvii, 54, 62, 64, 106, 109, 109–10, 111–12
  converting, 42–43
  death penalty, xix, 67–68, 97, 100
  exile, 67, 81
  infidels and, xviii–xix
  promises to, 52–53
  property rights, 66–67, 68–69, 81
  punishment, xix, 6, 62, 67–69, 97, 99, 102
  scandal, danger of, 53, 54, 61–62
  subversion, danger of, 53–54, 61–63

  toleration of, xvi–xviii, xix, xxix, xxxii, xxxiii–xxxiv, xxxv, 77, 86–87, 105
  treaties with, xxi–xxii, 55–59, 105–6
  waging war with, 89–91
  wickedness, 52–53, 54
  worship, places of, 82–83, 84–85
heretics, early Christian, xxviii, 53, 54, 62, 78–79, 81
  Arius, Arians, 79, 81, 82–83, 84–85
  Donatists, xvii, xxviii, 79, 85–86
  Manichaeans, xxviii
Honorius, Emperor, 67
Höpfl, Harro, xii
Humphrey, Laurence (1527–1590), 98–99
Hungary, 80
Hus, Jan (1369–1415), xiii, 96, 97–101, 106, 118
Hussites, 79

idolaters, 53–54, 62
infidels, xviii–xix, xxvii–xxviii, xxxii–xxxiii
injustice, 13, 15–16, 31, 55
  onerous contracts, 18–19, 20, 22, 24
Innocent III, Pope, 112
Isaac and Ishmael, 80
Isidore of Seville, 15
Israel, Jews, xxxi, xxxii–xxxii, 53–54, 80
Italy, 64

Jacob, 57–58, 80
James I of England, ix, xxx
Jerome of Prague (c. 1378–1416), 96, 100, 101–3, 106, 118

123

Index

Jesuits, Society of Jesus, ix–x, xiii, xxi, xxiv, xxxi, xxxv, 108, 116n23
  anti-Jesuit literature, xxv–xxvi, xxvii, 113–14
  Azor, Juan (1536–1603), 69
  Bellarmine, Robert (1542–1621), xiv, xv, xxx, xxxi, xxxii, xxxv, 72, 74
  Campion, Edmund (1540–1581), 98, 101
  contracts with heretics, xxv–xxvi, 106
  Duhr, Bernhard (1852–1930), xv
  equivocations, 113–16
  Gregory of Valencia (1549–1603), xvii, 69, 71, 74, 86
  Henríquez, Enrique (1546–1608), 63
  Lecler, Joseph (1895–1988), xv
  Lessius, Leonardus (1554–1623), 20, 116n23
  Mainz college, xivn16, xviiin24
  Maldonado, Juan (1534–1583), 87
  Molina, Luis de (1535–1600), x, xvii, 15, 16, 46, 86
  politiques and, xi, 3n1
  Ribadeneira, Pedro de (1527–1611), 3–4, 47
  Rosweyde, Heribert (1569–1629), xii–xiii
  Suárez, Francisco (1548–1617), 63, 64, 66
  Sweerts, Robert (1570–1646), xiii
Jesus Christ, 46–47, 90, 96, 112
  freedom of religion, 78–79
  heretics, toleration of, 86–87
  jurisdiction, 109–10
Jews, xxxi, xxxii–xxxiii, 53–54
John Chrysostom, 84–85

Joshua, xii, 55–56, 91
Jovian, Emperor, 81
Judah, 80
Judas, 99
Julian the Apostate, 80
Julius II, Pope, 107
Junius, Franciscus, xxxiv–xxxvn79
justice, 93, 97–98, 101–2
  judges, 115–16
  trials, 114–16
  virtue of, 33, 35, 47–48, 90
Justinian legal codes, 14n4, 15, 67
  Code, 15, 20, 45, 67, 81
  contracts, 12n8, 15, 22, 25
  Digest, 12n8, 14, 19, 20, 25, 46
  Institutes, 19
  promises, 19–20, 46
Justinian II, 72n4

Laban, 80
Lateran Council, 107
law, 114–16
  civil, 16, 19m 68
  divine, xvi, xvii, xxviii–xxix, 15, 38, 40–42, 46–47, 55, 110
  general, 93–95, 97, 100–103, 107
  natural law, 15, 18–19, 21–22. 30, 61–62, 64
  particular, 93, 95–97
  positive, 18–19, 25–26
  Roman, xi, 12n8, 14–15, 20, 23, 25, 81–82
  strict, 22–23
Lecler, Joseph (1895–1988), xv
Leo the Great, Pope, xxxix, 85
Leo X, Pope, 101, 107
Lessius, Leonardus (1554–1623), 20, 116n23
Levi, 57–58
licit (*licitum*), xl, 15, 17, 55
  lies as, 38, 41–42

lies, lying, 39–40, 115–16
  Bible on, 38, 40–42
  deception, 38–39, 42, 114
  devil and, 40–41
  evil, naturally, 42–43
  heretics, converting, 42–43
  Jesuits, 114–15
  as licit, 38, 41–42
  as sin, 37–40, 41–44, 55
Lipsius, Justus (1547–1606), 3–6, 47, 80
Livy, 5
Loefenius, Michael (1550–1620), xiii–xiv
Lutherans, 100
  Augsburg Confession, xxx
  Austrian, xvi, xxx, xxxi, 108
  toleration of, xxx–xxxi, xxxi
Luther, Martin, 15, 54, 95–96, 101

Machiavellians, xi, 3n1, 3n2, 3–4n3
Mainz, ix–x, xiii–xiv, xviii
Manichaeans, xxviii
Manuale controversiarum huius temporis, ix–x, xivn16, xx, xxxii, xxxv
Marcian, Emperor, 67–68
Marcus Antistius Labeo, 12n8
Mariana, Juan de, xxiv
marriage, 18, 22, 25
  adultery, 73–75
  contracts, xx, 18, 25, 71–75
  fidelity, 73–75
  to heretic, excommunicated, 62, 65
Martin V, Pope, 63, 64
Maximilian of Bavaria, xxx
Medina, Juan de (1490–1546), 26
miracles, 56, 58
mistakes, 19, 21, 23–25, 46

Molanus, Johannes (1533–1585), xvii–xviii, 6, 95, 101
Molina, Luis de (1535–1600), x, xvii, 15, 16, 45, 86
morals, xi, xvi, 16, 28
mortal sin, 28, 99
  lying, 37–38
  faithlessness, 44–47
  perjury, 48–49
  rights of others, violating, 45, 47–48
Moses, 80
Murad II, Sultan, 58
murders of clergymen, 63, 64
Mynsinger von Frundeck, Joachim (1514–1588), 93–94

natural law, 15, 30
  contracts, 18–19, 21–22
  heretics, 61–62, 64
Nauclerus, Johannes (c. 1430–1510), 98
Dr. Navarrus. *See* Azpilcueta, Martín de (1492–1586), Dr. Navarrus
Nebuchadnezzar of Babylon, 57
Netherlands, Dutch Republic, xii–xiii, 117
  Brederode, Pieter Cornelis van (ca. 1559–1637), xiv, xxi–xxiv, 105
  Palatinate, xxvi–xxvii
  Protestant, xix, xxi–xxiii, xxii
  Spain and, xx–xxii, 105–6, 108
  Twelve Years' Truce (1609–1621), xx–xxi
Neri, Philip (1515–1595), 82n8
Nicaean faith, 81
Nicholas, Pope, 110–12

125

Index

Oath of Allegiance, ix, xivn16, xxiiin40, xxx
oaths, 9, 12, 27–32, 67, 99
  dispensation by prince, 30–32
  God and, 27–28, 30, 31, 35, 48–49, 56
  promises under, 9, 12, 27–32, 33–34, 49, 90–91
  relaxation of, 29–32
offer, xl, 11–12
onerous promises, 9, 12, 17–25, 33–34, 35, 49
  contracts, 18–19, 20, 22, 24, 48
Origen, 41

pagans, 53–54, 55–56
Palatinate, xiii, xxi, xxi, xxvi–xxvii, xxx
Palud, Pierre de la (1275–1342), 18
Panormitanus, Abbas (Niccolò de' Tedeschi 1386–1445), 65
Pareus, David (1548–1622), xiv, xxvi, xxvi–xxix, xxxv
Paul VI, Pope, 98n23
Paul, apostle, 42, 53, 54, 62, 78
peace, 80, 117–18
  treaties, 105–6, 108, 116–17
Peace of Augsburg, xii, xxvii
perjury, xxv, 5–6, 31–32, 48–49, 55, 108
Peter, apostle, 110, 111
Peter Lombard, 18n3, 44n20, 62
Pharisees, 8–9, 46, 96
Philipp III of Spain, xxi
Pilate, Pontius, 8, 96
pious competition, xxxiii–xxxiv
Plancius, Daniel (ca. 1580–1618), xii–xiii
Plato, 41

Poland, 58, 80
political agreements, xii–xiv, xii–xiv, 5, 8
peace treaties, 105–6, 108, 116–17
politiques, xi, xii, 3–6
popes, power of, 109–12
  civil, 110–13
Portugal, 29
positive law, contracts, 18–19, 25–26
prayer, 62
Prem, Peter (Petrus Bremus), 95
Priscillianists, 41
promises (*promissio*), xi, xiii, xl, 8–9, 11–12, 45, 48
  cease of obligation, 51–52
  gratuitous, 9, 12, 13–16, 24, 33–34, 49
  to heretics, 52–53, 55
  Justinian legal codes, 19–20, 46
  moral obligation, xvi, 33–35, 45, 55
  onerous, 9, 12, 17–25, 33–34, 35, 49
  scholasticism, 12n8, 14, 34
  under oath, 9, 12, 27–32, 33–34, 49, 90–91
Protestants, xiii–xiv
  Anglicans, ix, xxx, 98n23, 99n28
  Calvinists, xii–xiii, xxiii, xxxi, 62, 79–80, 98, 100
  Calvin, John, 15, 54
  Catholics and, xn2, xi, xxv, xxvii, 105, 108, 114, 117
  Hus, Jan (1369–1415), xiii, 96, 97–101, 106, 118
  Jerome of Prague (c. 1378–1416), 96, 100, 101–3, 106, 118
  Lutherans, xvi, xxx, xxxi, 100, 108
  Luther, Martin, 15, 54, 95–96, 101

INDEX

Palatinate, xiii, xxi, xxi, xxvi–xxvii, xxx
See also Reformed Protestantism
Pseudo-Aristotle (Anaximenes of Lampsacus), 6
punishment, xix, 6, 62, 67–69, 97, 99, 102

rape, 18, 57
Reformed Protestantism, ix, xiv, xxiii
   in Europe, xiii–xiv, xxi, xxvi
   Junius, Franciscus, xxxiv–xxxvn79
   Palatinate, xiii, xxi, xxii
   Pareus, David (1548–1622), xiv, xxvi, xxvi–xxix
regicide, xxiv, xxx–xxxi
religion, virtue of, 33–34, 35, 48–49, 90
Ribadeneira, Pedro de (1527–1611), 3–4, 47
Richard of Middleton (Richard de Mediavilla c. 1249–c. 1308), 44
rights of others, violating, 45, 47–48, 55
rights, property, 66–69, 81
Roman Empire, 79, 81
Roman law, xi, 12n8
   contracts, xin6, 20, 23, 25
   freedom of religion, 81–82
   gratuitous promises, 14–15
   See also Justinian legal codes
Rosweyde, Heribert (1569–1629), xii–xiii
Rudolph, Emperor, 117

safe conduct, 93–98, 100–103, 107, 118
   general law, 93–95, 97, 100–103, 107
   particular law, 93, 95–97

Salamanca, 14n4, 15n13, 18n3, 19n5, 23n16, 26n28, 28n3, 31n8, 34n1, 44n21, 69n30, 115n18
Salatowsky, Sascha, xv
salvation, xvii, xx, 28, 43, 53, 78
Sanders, Nicholas (Sanderus, c. 1530–1581), 99
Saul, King, 56–57
Saxons, 94–95
scandal, danger of, 53, 54, 61–62
Scheid, Johann Georg (Georgius Scheidius), 58
scholastic, scholasticism, xviii–xix, xxixn63, 116n23
   promises, 12n8, 14n3, 34
   Spanish, x, xin6, 14n4
Schoppe, Caspar (1576–1649), xxv
Schreiner, Klaus (1931–2015), xv
Schwalbach, xxii, xxvi
Seneca, 4
Sergius, Pope, 72
Shechemites, 57–58
Sigismund, Emperor (1368–1437), 97–98, 100, 101–2, 106, 118
Silius Italicus, 4, 5
Simeon, 57–58
sin, 15–16, 27–28, 33, 65
   lie, as sin, 37–40, 41–44, 55
   mortal, 28, 37–38, 44–47, 48–49, 99
   venial, 28, 37–38, 43–45, 47–49
Soto, Domingo de (1495–1560), 18, 21, 44, 63, 69, 111
Spain, xx–xxi, xxx, 64
   Albert and Isabella, 105
   Castile, kingdom of, 29–30, 45
   king, as heretic, 106, 117–18
   Netherlands (lower Germany) and, xx–xxii, 105–6, 108
   Philipp III, xxi

scholastics, x, xin6, 14n4
Twelve Years' Truce (1609–1621), xx–xxi
Speckhan, Eberhard (1550–1627), 94, 103
Stapleton, Thomas (1535–1598), 98n24
Stieve, Felix, xiii–xiv
stipulations, 11–12, 22–23, 45–46
strict law, 22–23
Suárez, Francisco (1548–1617), 63, 64, 66
subversion, danger of, 53–54, 61–63
Sutcliffe, Matthew (d. 1629), xxiin40
Sweerts, Robert (1570–1646), xiii
Sylvester Prierias (Silvester Mazzolini da Prierio, 1456–1523), 28, 44, 46, 69, 115

Terence, 7
Theodoret of Cyrus, 84–85
Theodosius, Emperor, 67, 112
Theognides, 81
Thomas Aquinas, x, xvii, xviii–xix, 7, 35, 52
  infidels, xix, xxxii–xxxiii
  heretics, 62, 68, 71, 86, 89
  justice, 47, 115
  lies, 37–38
  vows, oaths, 11, 13, 31, 34, 48
Thucydides, 5
Thyraeus, Petrus (1546–1601), xviii
Tibullus, 6
tolerance, xiv–xvi, xxxvi
  early modern Europe, x, xiv–xv, xxxvi–xxxviii
  tolerance, religious, xviii–xix, xxxiv
    greater evil, xvii–xix, xxvii, xxviii, xxx, xxxii
    greater good, xxxi–xxxiii, xxxv, 86
    of heretics, xvi–xviii, xix, xxix, xxxii, xxxiii–xxxiv, xxxv, 77, 86–87, 105
    of Jews, xxxi, xxxii–xxxii
    limited, xxxii–xxxiii
    pious competition, xxxiii–xxxiv
    political motivation, xxi–xxii
    universal, xxvii–xxviii
transconfessional doctrine of contract, xxxvii
treaties (*foedus*), xl
  faith, keeping, xii–xiv, xii–xiv, 5, 8, 105–6
  with heretics, xxi–xxii, 55–59, 105–6
  Joshua and Gibeonites, xii, 55–56, 91
  peace, 105–6, 108, 116–17
Trent, Council of, xiin11, 29, 74, 95, 96, 107
truth, 39–40, 114–15
  lie, as sin, 37–40, 41–44
  virtue of, 33–34–35, 37, 90
Turks, xxi, xxxiv, 58–59,
  Catholics and, 106, 116–17
Twelve Years' Truce (1609–1621), xx–xxi
tyrannicide, xxiv, xxx–xxxi

Ulpian, 11, 35, 48
unjust cause, 89, 91
Urban II, Pope, 67

Valentinian, Emperor, 67–68, 82–83
venial sin, 28, 37–38, 43–45, 47–49
Venice, Republic of, xxxiv
Vienna, xxviii, xxxv

Vio, Tommaso de. *See* Cajetan, Cardinal (Tommaso de Vio, 1469–1534)
Vladislav III of Poland and Hungary, 58
von Hagen, Johann Ludwig, x
vows, 11, 65

war, 5, 89–91, 117–18
Whitaker, William (1548–1595), 98
Windeck, Johann Paul (d. 1620), xviii
Wycliffe, John, 99

Zedekiah, King, 57
Zipporah, 80

SOURCES IN EARLY MODERN ECONOMICS, ETHICS, AND LAW

Titles Available in the Second Series

On the Law of Nature: A Demonstrative Method
Niels Hemmingsen

On the Duty to Keep Faith with Heretics
Martinus Becanus

Titles Available in the First Series

A Treatise on the Alteration of Money
Juan de Mariana

On the Law in General
Girolamo Zanchi

On Law and Power
Johannes Althusius

On Exchange and Usury
Thomas Cajetan

On Righteousness, Oaths, and Usury: A Commentary on Psalm 15
Wolfgang Musculus

On Exchange: An Adjudicative Commentary
Martín de Azpilcueta

A Treatise on Money
Luis de Molina

The Mosaic Polity
Franciscus Junius

Of the Law of Nature
Matthew Hale

On Sale, Securities, and Insurance
Leonardus Lessius

www.ingramcontent.com/pod-product-compliance
Lightning Source LLC
Chambersburg PA
CBHW030328100526
44592CB00010B/611